A Journey into North America's
Vanishing Wilderness

FORESTS

FORESTS

A Journey into North America's
Vanishing Wilderness

Tim Fitzharris

Drawings by Don Li-leger

Wooded hillside near Montebello, Quebec.

Published in Canada in 1991 by
Stoddart Publishing Co. Limited
34 Lesmill Road
Toronto, Canada
M3B 2T6

Canadian Cataloguing in Publication Data
Fitzharris, Tim, 1948-
    Forests

Includes bibliographical references.
ISBN 0-7737-2498-2

1. Forest ecology — Canada.   2. Forest ecology —
United States.   3. Forests and forestry — Canada.
4. Forests and forestry — United States.
5. Wilderness areas — Canada.   6. Wilderness
areas — United States.   7. Photography — Land-
scapes.   I. Title.

QH86.F58 1991   574.5'2642'0971   C91-093748-6

Produced by Terrapin Books

Printed in Korea by Dong-A Printing Company

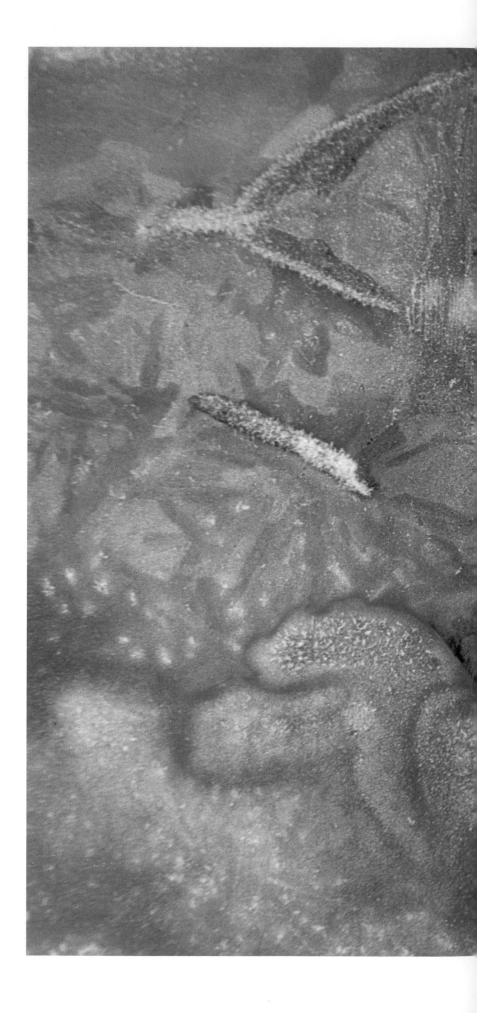

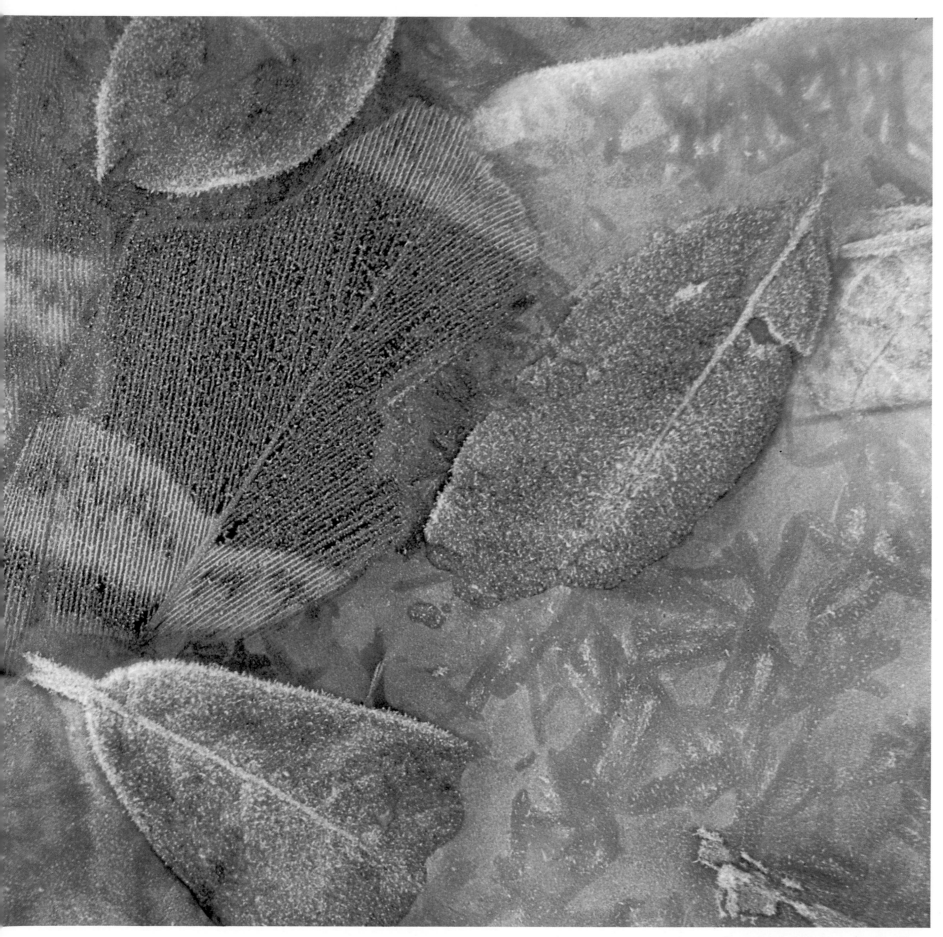

Frosted grouse feather and willow leaves.

There is no quiet place in the
white man's cities.
No place to hear the unfurling
of leaves in the spring,
or the rustle of insects' wings . . .
And what is there to life
if a man cannot hear the lonely
cry of the whippoorwill
or the argument of frogs around
the pool at night? . . .
Whatever befalls the earth
befalls the sons of the earth.

CHIEF SEATTLE

Sugar maples and American hornbeam along Mad River, Vermont.

In Memory of Jim Fitzharris

Bur oak, box elder, and trembling aspen near Chicago, Illinois.

Books by Tim Fitzharris

The Island
The Wild Prairie
The Adventure of Nature Photography
British Columbia Wild
Wildflowers of Canada with Audrey Fraggalosch
Canada: A Natural History with John Livingston
Wild Birds of Canada
American Birds
The Audubon Society Guide to Nature Photography

Western red cedars, Oliphant Lake, Vancouver Island.

Acknowledgments

For helping with logistics while traveling, for providing information on notable trees or forests, for advice on the manuscript, for support in other ways: Ora Beckett, Andrew Bryant, Lang Elliot, John Farrand Jr., Erma Fitzharris, Pat and Nat Fitzharris, Sheryl Fitzharris, Eric Fraggalosch, Helen Fraggalosch, Esther Houston, Don and Cora Li-Leger, Gordon and Kate Sherman. Most of all, Audrey Fraggalosch.

Tim Fitzharris

Giant sequoias, Yosemite National Park, California.

Table of

Contents

Second-growth red alder and Douglas-fir, Sudden Valley, Washington.

Preface

Red alder trunks, Sudden Valley, Washington.

AS A PHOTOGRAPHER, you become accustomed to seeing the world in terms of its pictorial merit. You drive down a high-way, and your eye frames a bank of clouds, a cluster of umbrellas at a bus stop, or a pond filled with water lilies. Subconsciously you judge the intensity of color, the depth of shadow, the geometry of shape, the interplay of content and concept. Sometimes you stop and take pictures. It often happens that a particular subject repeatedly evokes this process of picture-taking. You're not sure where the urge comes from, nor, at first, where it might lead. But the intrigue persists. For more than 10 years, photographing trees has been a major focus of my work. During this time few of these pictures were ever published. But that had no effect on my enthusiasm, and I continued to add new photographs of trees and forests to my collection.

For the first few years, I concentrated on showing interwoven patterns of trunks and leaves that become obvious when you record a piece of the forest in isolation, which is easy to do with a telephoto lens. Later on, thinking this approach too narrow, I began to photograph trees using a more varied selection of lenses, especially wide-angle focal lengths, to give the images more perspective, more the feeling of deep landscape. I explored other variations — shooting at sunrise or sunset to show how the trees reflected light, or recording forests against a backdrop of snow-capped mountains or along a frothy stream. For a while I worked at portraying the forest as partner to the sky, especially skies filled with heavy, brooding clouds.

Hundreds of rolls of film were spent exploring these themes. My interest in trees as a photographic subject remained strong, but I began to feel that my approach had been too egocentric, too tied to technique and my own desire to be creative. I hadn't given enough attention to the trees themselves.

It occurred to me that if you flattened out the forest, looked at it as if it were pasted on a canvas, forgot that what you were looking at were trees, leaves, and plants that you could climb or walk beneath, then you could consider a forest scene as an abstract painting. You would be looking at an expression of color, shape, line, and texture.

If I looked at the forest in this way and imagined the art piece hanging in a gallery somewhere, as I stood, relaxed in front of it, I discovered that I was looking at a work of genius. Sometimes, the artist seemed depressed, his palette weighed down with gray and brown. At other times, he would be exuberant, and the canvas would be flushed with fresh green or all the hues of a bonfire. But the works invariably showed depth, confidence, tension, surprise; each a universe packaged for the eye.

So I simplified my approach. I began to point and shoot. I pointed my camera at forests, or trees, or parts of trees, cropping out skies, streams, and mountains. I used lenses that didn't impose their optical bias on the scene. I shot on overcast days when the light was soft and even, and it rendered colors impartially and expressed shapes and textures without exaggeration. I relaxed and trusted in the beauty of my subject. It seemed to work. At least the photography stepped back and the trees and forests came forward. They are what this book is about.

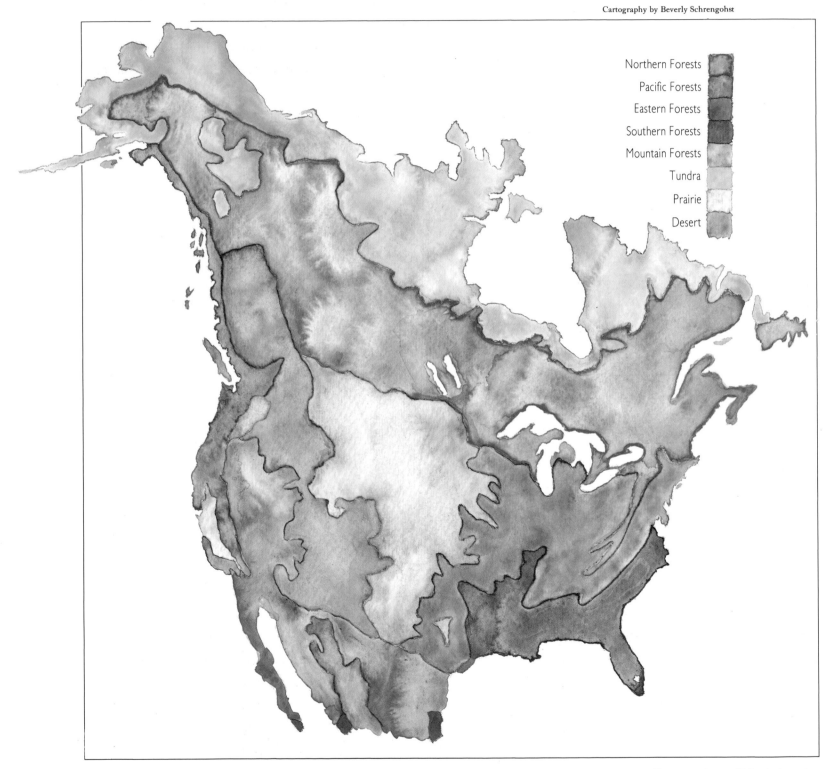

Cartography by Beverly Schrengohst

Northern Forests
Pacific Forests
Eastern Forests
Southern Forests
Mountain Forests
Tundra
Prairie
Desert

Forest regions of North America.

INTRODUCTION
Metamorphosis

FROM MY CHAIR on the porch I can see the butterflies. It's about noon and it's hot, more so now than when the vacant lot next door was shaded by hemlocks and firs. The trees were taken down to make room for a house that has yet to be built. Meanwhile the weeds and butterflies have taken over, replacements for the chickadees and bushtits that threaded through the thick branches that once hung in front of the upstairs windows.

The thistles are bathed in yellow light. The butterflies, white, brown, and orange, hover about the pink flowers. Two of them spiral upward in courtship: a swirl of hormones tossed against the sky. They are conscious only of each other. Soon the female will lay a row of eggs on the underside of a leaf.

I wouldn't miss the trees as much if the meadow wasn't just a sign of society catching its breath, of a temporary lull in the local housing market. But the bulldozer that cleared the trees lies waiting inside a chainlink fence somewhere nearby, and soon it will return, and there will be a lawn and a driveway and no more butterflies.

At one time, the trees along the north Pacific coast grew in unbroken stands, like stalks of new grass after a fire, their limbs thrusting toward the sky. They clothed the slopes of mountain chains and volcanoes; they sent their roots into naked cracks along high ridges; they stretched their boughs across rivers and into the pathways of glaciers.

The tallest forests lined the river valleys and deltas and crowded protected shorelines. Shielded from storms and inland frosts, they created a skyline no less than have the cities — Seattle and Vancouver — that later replaced them. Some trees rose nearly 30 stories — a marriage of earth and sky, of air and water, that had survived a thousand years.

The sun powered sap through this complexity of limbs and trunks. Wind bathed the leaves with sea mists and brought water sponged from the Pacific for the roots. Seeds were planted by red squirrels and

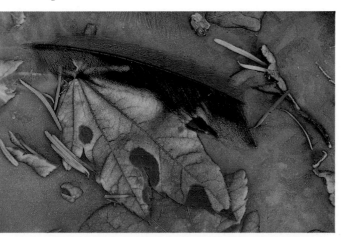

Vine maple leaves and Steller's jay feather, Washington.

Steller's jays and fertilized by black-tailed deer and Roosevelt elk. Raccoons occupied nests among the upper branches, and during long winter rains they shared their dreams of spring with the waiting trees.

In autumn, monarch butterflies migrated south to escape the wet and cold — a journey of many weeks. Each knew the route to the wintering grounds in southern California before it had broken from the chrysalis. The first part of their journey carried them over the rainforests that grew along Puget Sound. They floated past sculpted columns: old Douglas-firs deeply furrowed, red cedars with bark hanging in tattered strips, Sitka spruces shimmering with a thousand scales. The trunks were hard, like the stretched skin of a drum, and solid, but without the judgment of rock.

Near the day's end, the butterflies descended into the forest, passing through curtains of lichens and swooping over mosses that cushioned limbs and rotting stumps. They siphoned food from holes bored by sapsuckers in red alder and bitter cherry trees. After a storm, when sap leaked from wounds torn open by the wind, they feasted together and fell into heavy sleep as the owls began sounding.

The owls called through the night, a spill of soft energy from the dark corners of the forest. It rolled down live oak and sycamore canyons, swept across marshes, and nudged through groves of willow and cottonwood. The owls pronounced in furry accents, sometimes hissing, sometimes wailing, sometimes

barking like a sore dog. For millions of years they had talked to one another in this fashion.

In the beginning, the destruction of the forests spread slowly. Even a hundred years ago, the scars were scarcely noticeable among the mountain ranges and along the stretching coastline. But as more people settled and raised families, as the villages at the mouths of rivers spread into cities, as the demand for lumber grew, the assault on the forests accelerated. The landscape was to become a patchwork of gray, eroded earth, of manufactured second-growth tracts, and of virgin forests under sentence.

Armies of workers and machines were recruited. Roads were built to the edge of the forest. Even though only the largest trees were needed, nothing was spared. The workers knocked down slender saplings. They bulldozed snags and decaying trunks whose cavities were nurseries for bears and owls. They trampled ferns and fungi, and hacked through shrubs and seedlings — salmonberry, devil's club, salal, Oregon grape, rhododendron, ocean spray, thimbleberry, Indian plum, red-flowered currant, honeysuckle, dogwood, cascara, alder, vine maple, and madrone.

Finally one of the great trees would stand alone; naked in the sunlight for the first time in 10 centuries. Its beauty made the loggers hesitate. But they were impelled by an instinct much older than even the trees, and they unleashed their chain saws and severed the trunk.

The tree would shudder, twist slightly, and with a rush of wind and a quaking of land, it would come to rest where it had begun. But it was not left to sleep on the soft breast of the earth, to have its bruised body soothed by the fingers of red-cup fungus, tremellas, and puff balls.

Awed by its size, the workers swarmed along the length of the tree. Then they cut it up and took it away to sawmills or waiting ships. A few days later, they returned to torch the ruins of the forest, burning up what was left and blackening the earth. Cleared of debris, the soil was ready to nourish the seeds that would arrive on the wind and in the droppings of bear and grouse. In a few months, fireweed would transform the wasted terrain, inundating it with pink blossoms. It would be the first wave in a succession of plant communities leading to the restoration of the primeval forest. The process would take centuries.

THE DECIDUOUS woodlands east of the Cordillera suffered similar decline. More than 90 percent of them were cleared, mostly in the last century. They were replaced by farmlands, cities, and sprawling suburbs, and unending miles of roads bordered by nectar patches where a butterfly could grow fat.

These forests once spread without interruption from the Atlantic Ocean to the valley of the Mississippi. Here the trees distinguished each season with new pigments. By the time geese flew against the moon on cold nights, the green tones of summer had disappeared and the forests were washed with fire, as if all the butterflies in the world had landed at once to sleep.

In the North, winter gathered her forces over an expanse of conifers. As the days grew shorter, tamaracks shed their yellow needles, throwing sparks onto black bogs. The waters reflected skies busy with brown clouds and horizons dimmed by falling snow. In birch and willow thickets, bull moose were locked in combat — eyes rolled upward, velvet lips trailing

Giant sequoias and white firs, Yosemite National Park, California.

21

strings of saliva, bones and brains fused. Gray jays paused in branches above, ghostly quiet before the hot breathing and thin clatter of horns.

As the frost moved south, the sap shrank before it. The trees released their leaves to the wind, thin rags that sailed onto the decay below, scarlet and ocher mixing with the castings of fox and deer. The bare arms of maple, oak, basswood, beech, and sycamore remained above to shield the white sleep of the earth. Lines of wolves passing in front of the sun projected flickering blue shadows through gray trunks. Butterflies hung in lifeless hibernation beneath the loose bark of hickories and birches. Protected in cocoons, frozen caterpillars slept like small stones. Their relatives, the monarchs, rested far to the south, passing the cold months in the fir forests of Mexico. In late winter, they roused to accompany the sun northward on its return journey.

The monarchs were buoyed by warm winds laden with rain which washed and softened the earth, releasing plants that winter had locked in the soil. Bloodroots and skunk cabbages pushed through the thinning snow. Then trilliums, violets, dwarf irises, and orchids spread their petals in the sun. Each day saw new color in the forest — the white of blossoming cherries, dogwoods, and hawthorns, the pink and lavender of redbud, the mint of new foliage. The sun grew stronger, and soon the forest canopy was again in place. The land was green, roasting in indolent summer comfort, delirious with the buzz of grasshoppers by day and the chirp of crickets by night.

IT IS SUMMER now on the West Coast. The madrone and Douglas-firs that grew on the hillsides around my house have been replaced by houses like mine. Without the trees it is windier and

Staghorn sumac, daisies, and thistles near Cornwall, Ontario.

drier here, ideal habitat for wildflowers you would expect to find on the prairies.

The butterflies do not see the city's outline in the distance. But I notice that the air downtown thickens as the day passes. Hazes of yellow and gray stack up on the horizon. The sun bleeds through, a red disk staring at a forest of billboards and draping wires, of polished aluminum, neon tubing, glass, and concrete. Instead of the sound of wind in trees, a bristling static intones, blended from rolling vehicles, from jets, from radios, from buildings filled with machines.

I weigh the aesthetics of what has replaced the trees. The shapes of the buildings have a powerful

geometry. The textures are varied, yet formally organized. The interplay of angles and lines is intriguing. The color is nondescript, but I know that this will change come darkness. The city is not without beauty. But it is no more attractive than a woodland hung with a million oak leaves, each one different, yet all of them the same. And unlike the leaves and flowers of the woods, the city's blunt shapes and telescoping perspectives are lifeless. They do not speak to the people that pass through the shadows.

Nevertheless, I can appreciate the city's existence. For us, its value is greater than the forest that occupied this land. Where once a few men found sustenance, now thousands live amidst plenty. To us the city is beaver pond and bee hive. It is drumming log, termite mound, heron colony, grouse lek, spawning stream, calving ground, and nectar patch. But, it is too much.

In the lot next door, light plays on grasses, black-eyed Susans, chicory, and daisies. The patches of bull thistle and goldenrod swarm with bees and butterflies. Sometimes two or three feed side by side on the same flower head, rooting into the bundles of pistils and stamens, bumping into each other. They hover and flit, and change course without warning. But their industry is business-like, determined.

Overhead the mating butterflies hang on the currents. The eggs they are minting will launch new caterpillars. Fat, soft, accepting, and aimed at a magical metamorphosis, they will crawl and eat without regard. The forest, too, abides. It has seen mountain ranges rise and fall. It has been drowned by oceans and burnt by deserts. It has harbored dinosaurs, and for a short while, it has lived with man. Now, as cracks appear in the cocoon of time, as change flexes its wings for another foray, the forest watches the sun and talks with the wind.

Should you sit down, the great, dry, green sea would sweep over and engulf you. If you called out a thousand echoes would mock back. If you wrestle with the growth it will strike back. If you listen it will talk, if you jabber it will shut up tight, stay inside itself.

EMILY CARR
from *Hundreds and Thousands:
The Journals of an Artist*

Pacific Forests

Pacific Forests

OR MOST OF the winter they sit on the outstretched limbs of Douglas-firs, looking first to the left and then to the right. Then without apparent effort the song erupts, pushing through the clinging fog and the soaking vegetation. A sound the shape of a pillow, the color of a ripe peach, it reaches into the heavy gray green of the forest and for a few seconds you can remember what spring feels like. The varied thrush, its plumage the color of a jack-o-lantern, spends the winter in the rainy confines of the Pacific forests when most of its relatives have migrated southward. For a visitor to these woodlands, its song is uplifting, a trinket immersed in a sea of dark trees.

The furnishings in this habitat have the unmistakable aspect of monuments. Trunks loom like buildings, and a herd of Roosevelt elk moving through them seems tentative, fragile, lilliputian. The largest trees in an old-growth forest on

Vancouver Island have stood for more than 1,000 years, some of the giant sequoias in California for 2,500. In their presence, a human feels small and temporary.

The mosses, the carpet of fallen needles, the boughs and hanging lichens muffle sound. On entering the forest, you attend to the unaccustomed vacuum, to the sensation that something is about to happen. But with each step, you realize that this gloomy place holds few surprises, that it moves with ponderous calm, that it has swallowed you with little notice.

Of the earth's coniferous forests, those of the Pacific Coast of North America are the tallest and most luxuriant. Sandwiched between the Pacific Ocean and ice-capped mountain ranges, they are spread on a landscape no less dramatic. Stretching for 3,000 miles (4,800 kilometers) from Kodiak Island, Alaska to the Santa Cruz Mountains of California, they clothe the humid seaward slopes of a jumble of mountain ranges — the coastal ranges of Alaska, British Columbia, and central California; the Olympic Mountains of Washington, the Cascades in Washington, Oregon, and southern British Columbia; the Klamath Mountains of southwestern Oregon and northwestern California, and the Sierra Nevada Mountains of California.

The trees of the Pacific region owe their dimension to the ocean, which brings abundant moisture, and to mountain ranges, which protect their eastern flanks from arctic air masses originating inland. Some of the wettest places receive up to 120 inches (3 meters) of rain a year, most of it falling during the winter. Except in the Sierran forests, snow covers the ground for only a few days or weeks each year, if at all. Throughout the region, summers are dry and sunny. During this season, cool temperatures reduce the effects of drought, except in southern California where the mercury often surpasses 90 degrees Fahrenheit (32 degrees Celsius).

The Pacific forests contain three closely related but distinctive forest communities. In the southern part of the zone, the forests of coastal California are dominated by redwoods, which grow on lowlands and floodplains wherever there is persistent summer fog. The range of the redwoods ends abruptly a little north of the California-Oregon border. Thereafter, no single type of tree is prevalent, but four or five major species can be identified that characterize the old-growth forests to the north. The third major type of forest clothes the slopes and valleys of the Sierra Nevada Range of central California. It contains the earth's most diverse coniferous forests and its largest trees, the giant sequoias.

Unable to grow at elevations exceeding 2,700 feet (800 meters), the northern Pacific forests are largely confined to a strip of land 15-40 miles (24-64 kilometers) wide along the length of the coast.

Along major river valleys, they may extend inland as much as 90 miles (150 kilometers). They are dominated by western red cedar, Douglas-fir, western hemlock, Sitka spruce, and Pacific silver fir. In some stands there may be an even mixture of varieties, in others only one or two species prevail depending on local climate, topography, and the incidence of forest fires. Some of the best known remnants of virgin rainforest in the northern regions are found in the Tongass National Forest in Alaska, Pacific Rim National Park in British Columbia, Olympic National Park in Washington, and along the Rogue River in Oregon.

Easily recognized by its sweeping boughs and loose bark, the western red cedar was the life-giving tree for coastal Indians. Its bark was used for clothing and baskets, its branches were twisted into strong rope, its logs were stacked and fitted into spacious lodges, and its trunks were hollowed out to make ocean canoes with which the Indians hunted for whales and fished for salmon. It remains the most valuable species of the rainforest; its even-grained wood, naturally resistant to rotting, is used in many exterior building applications. Able to withstand high winds and fires, some of the oldest specimens claim a life span of more than 10 centuries. Red cedars also grow to enormous size. It takes more than 20 seconds to walk around one such giant on Meares Island in British Columbia.

Not as distinctive in appearance, but more wide-spread and abundant, is the western hemlock. As a seedling, this species grows quickly in deep shade, giving it an advantage over other trees competing for limited light. Even more efficient at making use of scarce light is the Pacific silver fir, but it is better adapted to wet terrain and is not as prevalent. Although not as large as the red cedar, both of these species reach heights of 180 feet (55 meters) and attain diameters of 5 feet (1.5 meters).

The Sitka spruce, more than any other species, distinguishes the Pacific forests. It grows to heights of 250 feet (76 meters), thriving on oceanside lowlands buffeted by salt spray and moist winds. Sometimes it forms pure stands, as on the Queen Charlotte Islands. In other places, it is mixed with Douglas-fir, red cedar, and western hemlock. Its trunk rises like a telephone pole, smooth and straight. Valuable to industry, the resilient wood is made into buildings, boats, musical instruments, and at one time, even aircraft super structures, including the "Spruce Goose" built by Howard Hughes.

Although other rainforest trees rival it in size, none seems as impressive as the Douglas-fir. Standing next to an old-growth specimen, you are first awed by its bark. The tough, rumpled tissue envelopes the tree in deep ridges. Often more than a foot thick, it carries the eye upward along dark furrows to the canopy.

There are places of interest along the way. Near the base of the trunk are artist fungi, stacked like shelves, clinging to the ridges, drawing sustenance from the bark which decays even while the tree lives. On one of the brackets a Douglas squirrel rests on its haunches. It spins a fir cone in front of its incisors, nipping off the seeds, and letting the bracts flutter to the ground. Its family has used this spot as a diner for years, and beneath the tree grows a midden of cone leftovers 3 feet (1 meter) thick and more than 10 feet (3 meters) in diameter.

The eye climbs higher into the transects of limbs. Here Steller's jays hop through the branches in search of insect larvae, proclaiming occasionally with a screech, squall, or sometimes a toot that they have no fear and know their business. A brown creeper twirls round the trunk, disappearing when it descends the ridges of bark to search out a grub. Others are likely to flit past — chestnut-backed chickadees in winter, Townsend's warblers in spring, and whispering flocks of waxwings in fall.

A shadow flickers above and pulls the eye quickly upward another 10 stories. A bald eagle has come to its nest. It rests momentarily, tongue splayed out, breast heaving, a white-winged scoter clamped in its talons. The scoter's gut is stuffed with blue mussels ripped from the seabed offshore. Another scoter carcass and a purple starfish are draped over the edge of the huge nest. At the base of the tree is more surplus — seabirds and the drying, twisting remains of fish.

GREEN FOR MOST of the year, the coast redwood forests of California and southern Oregon offer little else in the way of color. But this sliver of the spectrum has nooks worthy of notice. No green seems as pure as the wet leaves of bigleaf maple on an overcast day. The lichens that hang in hairy clumps are green, but barely so, and they are tinted with mint; the foliage of the redwoods is intensely green, but it glows inside a blue aura. Low in the understory, salal and rhododendron leaves are dark with chlorophyll tightly packed to reap the light that trickles into this stratum. In contrast, the older Douglas-firs lift their needles into the strongest light, where the green relaxes to near gray. There are other variations — the greens cast from ferns, mosses, shrubs, herbs, and grasses. The green of the forest is relieved in spring when rhododendrons thrust out their pink blossoms, and again in the fall when bigleaf maples turn dull gold and vine maples blood red.

During the summer, fog masks the color of the redwood forests. It slinks in from the sea, rolling off the surf, oozing through the cypresses and salmonberry that guard the shoreline. It pulses around the solid towers of trees, insulating them from the blue skies above, from the sun that can rob moisture from the leaves.

Stepping into these forests on a clear day in July, there is at first the feeling that somehow the trees have just arrived. Their size imposes, calling for silence, for a reconsideration of dimension. Just a few stories above the ground is the first cloud. Above that, more trees. The trunks begin to telescope, but it is not clear whether this is due to diminishing size or simply to intervening distance. A patch of blue is revealed, then obscured by a curtain of vapor. Still more trunks skewer the components together, stringing cloud and sky on a shaft of gray.

Ethereal though it may be, the fog is nonetheless prisoner of the rugged terrain that holds it in the shallow bays and fjords and shoves it up the river valleys. The mountains control the rain in a similar fashion, although with boundaries not so strict. The land thus creates distinct patterns of vegetation. With most of the precipitation moving in from the west, any upthrusting terrain causes the weather systems to rise, cool off, and lose their moisture. This drenches the seaward slopes and creates rainforests. It dries out those slopes which, due to a loop in a river valley, a bend in a fault line, or the rise of a volcano, happen to face inland. Here are open woodlands comprised mostly of oaks — deciduous species in dry areas, evergreen species on moist, frost-free sites, together with California laurel and madrone. Along water-courses grow ashes, alders, and willows. Much of the coastal region of California is covered with savanna — rolling grasslands scattered with oaks. In spring, the meadows are spread with California poppy and blue camas. But the blooming season gives way to drought, and by summer's end these woodlands have been scorched of their color and await the slaking of their thirst by winter rains.

Found inland from the redwood forests are the Sierran forests, which occupy the higher mountain ranges of the Pacific Coast region, from southern Oregon to Baja, California. These forests are diverse, with more than 24 species of conifers and a like number of deciduous trees. They also contain many record-sized trees, the result of a favorable climate. The trees enjoy a growing season seven months long. Winters are wet and mild, and summers are warm and dry with frequent droughts.

The composition of these forests depends on the degree of precipitation, which differs significantly with topography. Some stands are a mixture of conifers, with ponderosa pine at the lowest, driest elevations and Jeffrey pine in higher regions of heavier snow. The latter usually grow with varied mixtures of white fir, Douglas-fir, lodgepole pine, western white pine, sugar pine, and incense cedar. Pure stands of red fir frequently occur above the slopes of mixed conifers. The giant sequoia groves stake out their territories in cool, shaded enclaves of rich soil that remain moist throughout the summer dry season. Rocky, dry habitats are often claimed by California black oaks. Typical understory vegetation is similar to that found in the forests along the coast with the addition of giant chinkapin, tanoak, white alder, California laurel, and greenleaf manzanita.

POSITIONED ON THE horizontal limb of a sequoia, the spotted owl looks like a hand-shaped urn. Its talons flex inconspicuously. Its head swivels fluidly. A thin film of skin descends over one golf-ball-sized eye. The bird is hunting, and from 40 feet (12 meters) below, the soft sound of a deer mouse gathering seeds for its larder penetrates the darkness. The noise activates the nerves at the end of funnel-shaped receptors positioned on each side of the bird's head. One is larger than the other, allowing the owl to calculate, by sound alone, the distance to its prey.

The hunter drops from the perch and becomes a compact missile for a few milliseconds: it opens its wings briefly to adjust the trajectory, hurtles through the thin ceiling of manzanita, opens its wings again,

lowers its tail, and its talons have found the mouse. There is no struggle from the prey. It dies without a scream. And for the owl, there is no celebration. Its prey is but one of thousands it has swallowed. Owl, mouse, sequoia tree, and manzanita berries form an association millions of years old — a puzzle locked together with rain, fog, warm Pacific air, and with solitude.

Portfolio
Pacific Forests

Northern saw-whet owl.

THE EARTH'S largest conifers are found in the Pacific forests region where a temperate climate and abundant precipitation favor tree growth. Warm air from the Pacific Ocean rises on encountering the mountain ranges, cools rapidly, and releases its moisture over the coastal lowlands and west-facing slopes. In some areas, more than 100 inches (2.5 meters) of rain drench the forests each year.

Old-growth spruce and hemlock forest, Pacific Rim National Park, Vancouver Island.

Frosted vine maple and red alder leaves, North Cascades National Park, Washington.

Sitka spruce trunks, Carmanah Valley, Vancouver Island.

ALASKA CEDAR grows
in the upper reaches of the
Pacific forests, rarely being found
below 3,300 feet (1,000 meters). It has
distinctive bark, peeling off in strips
like that of western red cedar. Generally
a slender, slow-growing conifer, it sometimes requires more than 200 years to
reach full stature. Some gnarled
specimens only 5 feet (1.5 meters) in
diameter may actually be more than
1,000 years old. Alaska cedar is also
known as yellow cedar, which refers to
the color of the wood and the foliage.

Satin flower, Saltspring Island.

Alaska cedars, Coast Mountains, British Columbia.

Bigleaf maples, Mount Baker National Forest, Washington.

FEW DECIDUOUS trees are found in the Pacific forests. Of these, the bigleaf maple is the most prominent. It has the largest leaf of any North American maple, measuring more than a foot across. Although vine and Douglas maples are also native to the Pacific forest, only the bigleaf maple reaches tree size. It is shade-tolerant and thrives in moist soils. Its bark soaks up water, which encourages mosses, liverworts, ferns, and even other tree seedlings to grow on its trunk and larger branches.

AN OLD-GROWTH forest is special not only for the age and enormous size of the trees, but also for the diversity of plants, mammals, birds, and other animals that live there. The mature trees in an old-growth forest are hundreds of years old. Their trunks and limbs are covered with mosses and lichens. Those that are blown over by storms or toppled by disease become nurse logs for seedlings, which are nurtured by the moisture and nutrients in the decaying wood. Others remain standing even though they may have been killed by lightning or fire. They become infested with beetles and grubs, which are eaten by woodpeckers and nuthatches. The cavities that develop in their trunks become dens for bears, raccoons, and squirrels.

Douglas-firs and western hemlocks, Cathedral Grove, Vancouver Island.

Red alder grove, Redwood National Park, California.

*R*ED ALDER *is the most
abundant deciduous tree in the
Pacific forests region in areas that have
been clear-cut by logging or opened up
by fire or landslides. It occurs typically
in dense groves along watercourses
or wherever soils are moist and rains
frequent. Alder reseeds quickly, and its
saplings grow so fast that a clearing can
disappear in a few years. Eventually,
alders are replaced by longer-lived,
slower-growing conifers. Although
alder has limited commercial value, it
improves soils by adding nitrogen via
root nodules and humus through the
decomposition of leaves. As a result,
Douglas-fir and other conifers thrive
in the areas that they take over
from alders.*

AWAY FROM the coast, much of what may be considered rainforest consists of Douglas-fir. Monumental as this species may appear, it is not a climax tree, since the seedlings cannot grow in the shade of the parent trees. After about 10 centuries of growth, the mature specimens begin to weaken and eventually topple over, to be replaced by shade-tolerant western hemlocks and red cedars. Regular occurrence of forest fires since the last glacial invasion about 10,000 years ago, however, has created enough open landscape for the Douglas-fir to retain its widespread status.

Douglas-firs, Sudden Valley, Washington.

THE GIANT SEQUOIA grows at high elevations between 4,500-8,000 feet (1,370-2,400 meters) on the west slopes of the south and central Sierra Nevadas. Although not as tall as its relative, the redwood, the sheer bulk of this botanical behemoth makes it the world's largest living organism. The best known groves of giant sequoias are protected in Sequoia, Yosemite, and King's Canyon National Parks in California. Here you can wander among monolithic trunks over 2,000 years old and 20 feet (6 meters) in diameter. The tallest sequoias reach heights of more than 300 feet (91 meters), towering over their common associates, sugar pine, Douglas-fir, and white fir.

Giant sequoias, Mariposa Grove, Yosemite National Park, California.

Black bear scolding cub among Sitka spruce, western hemlock and western red cedar, Vancouver Island.

THE BLACK BEAR of the Pacific forests is generally larger than those found inland. This may be due to more abundant food supplies, particularly salmon. Adaptability to a wide range of habitats has made the black bear one of the most successful large carnivores in North America. It has few natural enemies except for man who kills about 30,000 bears every year. The black bear's tree climbing ability, perhaps developed in a long ago era when it was vulnerable to giant predators now extinct, is its best defense against wolves and grizzlies which may attack females and cubs.

Stream swirl below Sitting Lady Falls, Vancouver Island.

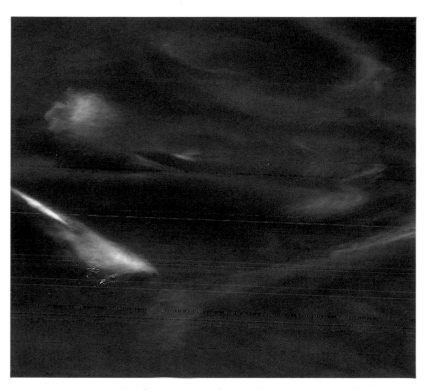

Swirling sockeye salmon, Skeena River, British Columbia.   *Autumn leaves and salmon, Ketchikan, Alaska.*

*E*VERY FALL, *coastal streams and rivers are littered with the carcasses of spawning salmon. The final stages of the salmon's life cycle are the most dramatic. After years in the open sea, adult fish swim toward land and pick out their natal stream from thousands. They head upstream, hurtling themselves over rocks and waterfalls, toward a gravel spawning bed. After the eggs are fertilized, the salmon die almost immediately. Their carcasses become food for eagles, gulls, crows, ravens, mink, bears, and raccoons. The forests that line these watercourses are vital in maintaining the clear water necessary for salmon reproduction. Rapid run-off of surface water, which occurs when trees are clear-cut, carries silt into streams and smothers salmon eggs.*

Black-tailed deer beneath madrone, Chuckanut Mountain, Washington.

A SUBSPECIES of mule deer, the black-tailed deer is the common deer of the Pacific forests. It has smaller antlers and lacks the distinctive white rump patch of inland races. Black-tails are well-adapted to coastal life, often swimming a few miles between islands to reach better forage. In winter, they seek shelter in heavily forested areas, browsing on Douglas-fir, western red cedar, Pacific yew, salal, and huckleberry. During spring and summer, does cache their fawns in heavy growth when away feeding, to safeguard them from predators.

This is a beauty
of dissonance,
this resonance
of stony strand,
this smoky cry
curled over a black pine
like a broken
and wind-battered branch
when the wind
bends the tops of the pines
and curdles the sky
from the north.

This is the beauty
of strength
broken by strength
and still strong.

A.J.M. SMITH
The Lonely Land

Northern Forests

Northern Forests

THE WOLVES GLANCE sidelong into the eyes of the cow moose as she struggles across the lake. It is frozen and covered with two feet of snow, not an impediment to the long legs of a moose, but enough to flounder a wolf. However, it is April and rain has fallen through the night, freezing on the snow. The cow moves slowly, stepping high. Each hoof must smash through the ice before reaching solid footing. For a few steps a rhythm builds, but sometimes the crust holds and the moose must bring her forequarters onto the surface; an uncertain hind leg follows. Then the crust collapses, staggering the moose and drawing the ring of wolves tighter.

The wolves have their own problems. Broad feet keep them moving easily on top of the ice, but a change in direction sends them into a skid. They prefer to attack from the rear, away from the moose's front hooves, immobilizing her by severing the hamstring. But none of the pack wants to leave the unbroken crust for the ragged ice chunks and deep snow in the moose's wake. Instead they trot alongside her, drooling and whining.

Trees loom in the distance — spruces, tamaracks, and pines — murky, colorless forms about 30 feet (9 meters) high that surround the lake like the wall of a bull ring. Tonight they will embrace the moose and turn away the blood hunt of the wolves.

As the moose nears the lakeshore, the crust grows thinner. Here the forest canopy catches the rain before it reaches the snow, and ice forms instead on the branches of the trees. It is salvation for the moose, as if a carpet had been lifted from the snow for her to slip under. She gains speed, hooves kicking up a shower of white. The branches shake and sway, closing together after her. She passes into the darkness of the forest. The wolves do not follow. Without the ice to walk on, they cannot keep up, and the lament begins.

It seems to come from deep within the ground, rising too smoothly amidst the clutter of crooked trees, of ragged lakes and bogs, and of unending miles of snow and ice. It wells up, clean and sure of its sadness, and spreads across the land, not an echo but a solid wail that sucks you into the blackness. The first howl provokes the others, and the wolves raise their long, hairy jaws, drawing thin lips over fangs to shape the sound, to slide its purple fullness into the vacuum of wilderness, to register a claim on this territory and on this moose that they will hunt again tomorrow.

The boreal forests are refuge for wolves and moose and other large animals that have declined in the rest of the continent. They are part of the northern forest region that stretches from Newfoundland westward for some 4,000 miles (6,400 kilometers), nearly to the Pacific Ocean. To the south, the northern forests are bounded by the aspen parkland of the prairies and the eastern deciduous forests south of the Great Lakes basin, with a single finger projecting down the spine of the Appalachian Mountains for 600 miles (960 kilometers) to Georgia's northern border.

Arctic tundra marks the northern extension of these forests. Beyond the last line of trees, wind and cold temperatures limit plant growth to ground-hugging grasses, mosses, herbs, shrubs, and stunted trees. It is a wandering boundary, shaped by soil and microclimate, with islands of trees found deep inside the tundra, just as there are patches of tundra interspersing the forest.

For all its area (equal to North America's other forest zones combined), the boreal forest has little variation. There are but a handful of tree species, mostly conifers mixed with birches, willows, and aspen. None of them grows to impressive size. The deciduous species do not set ablaze the fall woodlands like their southern counterparts. There is a monotony to the short growing season, to the relentless winters, to the poor, acidic soils, to the unending ranks of sticklike trees, to the pervasive gray-green silence interrupted infrequently by the call of a loon or the fall of a spruce cone.

White and black spruces are the dominant species of conifer. Black spruce is well adapted to the wet, poorly drained terrain so abundant in the north. It lines the shores of lakes and bogs, often leaning drunkenly this way or that, the result of heaving frost. An upland variety also grows well on dry granite ridges. Black spruce has a swollen crown and is smaller than the white spruce with which it often associates. The latter prefers higher ground, where drainage is better. It reaches heights up to 140 feet (43 meters) and trunk diameters 4 feet (1.2 meters) at maximum size. The bark of both species — thin and sinuous, with resinous secretions — provides little defense against fire, a handicap less for the black spruce, protected as it is by wet habitat.

Other conifers are less important, though they may be widespread. Jack pine, the most northern of American pines, is a pioneering species that can quickly reseed areas cleared by fire or logging. The broad, shallow root system of the tamarack is suited to poorly drained soils. Its range extends to treeline and, in dwarfed form, beyond.

Although much of the boreal zone is comprised of lakes and rocky uplands covered with reindeer moss and shrubs, its most distinguishing feature is muskeg. There are hundreds of thousands of square miles of it: a terrain built of decomposing, water-logged sphagnum mosses and other plant debris. Each footstep here creates a big dimple that fills immediately with water and offers the support of jello. These boggy areas, made acidic in part by falling needles, are invariably rimmed by black spruce and tamarack. Scrub willows and birches are common ground cover along with small cranberry, Labrador tea, and swamp laurel. The latter two have adapted to the cold, dry winds by growing a layer of insulating hairs on the undersurface of their leaves.

The boreal forests are the least diverse of North America's woodlands. Nevertheless, they are home to about 26,000 different species, including 50 trees, 58 mammals, 200 birds, thousands of insects, and between 1,200 and 2,200 flowering plants and even more fungi. However, the conception of the North as an uninhabited wilderness of unending forests, pristine lakes, and abundant wildlife is an anachronism. Human industry now jeopardizes this.

The long fibers of mature white and black spruce make the highest quality paper in the world. When such forests are clear-cut, as many of them have been, they are naturally replaced by aspen. The creamy xylem of aspen also makes good paper — smooth, ultra-white, and non-yellowing — and this species too has been widely harvested by northern pulp mills. Although governments have not monitored the depletion, it is estimated that 65 percent of commercially productive virgin forest has been lost. In the past 10 years, Canadian industry has razed a forest the size of East Germany; encouraged by tax concessions and subsidies, the rate of cutting is steadily increasing.

FARTHER SOUTH the wind blows warmer year-round. It supports a hawk which sails above a canopy of broad leaves. Her wings are stretched flat. Not in a hurry, she works the currents for the momentum needed to reach her nest. A tailwind pushes her faster, infusing the pound of muscle, tendon, and foamy bone with kinetic energy. Suddenly she raises a wingtip, tilts a broad row of striped tail feathers, and banks into the wind. Flung into a smooth turn, she skirts the wall of a white pine looming 30 feet (9 meters) above the rest of the canopy. She rolls sideways, loses all wing lift, and slips quickly into the dense forest, knifing through a maze of limbs and leaf clumps without ruffling a feather. She rights herself, glides on outstretched wings for a second, and then spreads her primaries to catch the air. Tail lowered and fanned, talons thrust forward, she flaps for the first time to absorb the shock and lands. She stares into her nest, securely wedged against the beech trunk. It is decorated with green sprays of pine and humped with a fuzzy pile of young.

The broad-winged hawk makes its home in the southern reaches of the northern forest, where an extensive transition zone, centered about the Great Lakes-St. Lawrence River system, is distinguished from the boreal forests by an invasion of broad-leaved trees. The broad-winged hawk hunts in the understory of this forest, perching quietly on the low limb of a sycamore or boxelder near a pond, looking for toads, large insects, or even red squirrels that may be foraging for mushrooms. The hawk's forest home has boundaries, for most of the transition forest area was settled and cleared of trees long ago. Only five percent has been left undisturbed.

This forest is composed primarily of sugar maple and beech. Elsewhere yellow birch and basswood are plentiful where they replace the beech to form dominant associations with sugar maple. Transition forests may be interspersed with eastern hemlock, balsam fir, jack pine, and eastern white cedar, growing singly or in groves. However, eastern white pine is chief among the conifers and thrives in areas disturbed by fire. Boreal species are present too — paper birch, trembling aspen, spruce, and tamarack — but they no longer dominate and are most likely to be found along high ridges, on shaded, north-facing slopes, or near bogs and swamps.

The understory is filled with the saplings of climax species, waiting for storms or disease to bring down the limbs that form the canopy above, to open an avenue to the sun, to provide them a chance to reach full size. There are smaller species — white ash, black cherry, and flowering dogwood — that have no aspirations for the canopy. They live in the shadows, sustained by the weak light that passes through the close net of leaves above. A profusion of shrubs, ferns, and wildflowers completes the understory, a crowded world where sound is often more telling than sight.

The springtime drumming of the ruffed grouse is an announcement of territorial claim and amorous intent. It leaks through the vegetation, a warm patter soothing to the ear that leaves off just before its rising intensity begins to intrude. Other birds proclaim their amorous desires: the ovenbird's insistent *tea-cher, tea-cher, tea-cher*, the northern parula's rising, buzzy trill that reverses itself to end abruptly in a descending *zip*, the acadian flycatcher's explosive *pit-zee*. The woofing of a startled black bear, the thumping to the ground of pine cones snipped off by a squirrel — the repertoire is unending, and seldom can its sound be coupled with the sight of the performer.

Before European settlement the mixed forests were the domain of the eastern white pine. It associated with other trees or grew in pure stands, attaining heights exceeding 250 feet (75 meters) and diameters of 6 feet (1.8 meters). After California's sugar pine, it was the continent's largest pine and our most important timber tree for almost 300 years. It was used for ship's masts, furniture, buildings, fuel, for practically anything that required wood. By the turn of the century, the virgin stands were depleted, and today all of the giant pines are gone and specimens exceeding even 100 feet (30 meters) are uncommon. Now the trees of the mixed forest region face a new and insidious threat, one no less lethal than a chain saw.

THE SPRING RAINS had been heavy, and sitting quietly on her eggs, the cerulean warbler paid no notice to the yellow pigments creeping into the maple leaves about her nest. The color spread, and soon the leaves no longer presented themselves to the sun but clung limply to their stems. By the time the nestlings began to exercise their wings, some of the nearby twigs were bare, exposing the birds to weather and predators.

When summer arrived, the warblers had disappeared. The maple continued to yellow and lose foliage, so that its announcement of autumn was made without the usual drama. Rains came and went, seasons passed, and the tree grew weaker. Each spring it mustered fewer leaves in clumps more isolated among the clattering limbs. As if sensing the end, one autumn the maple produced an abundance of seeds. Its limbs had lost their strength, and one by one they were sheared off by wind and snow. A few years after the first leaves had sickened, a pair of warblers reappeared. They rested for a while on the trunk, which by then was all that remained, and then flew on.

Acid rain is believed to have killed thousands of trees in the mixed forests. It forms from sulphur dioxide, released in the millions of tons annually from the smokestacks of power plants, smelters, and other heavy industries. The emissions may travel hundreds of miles on the wind before combining with water molecules to form acid rain. But sulphur dioxide may not be the only culprit. Evidence suggests that other pollutants, such as vehicle exhaust, which enter the forest ecosystem in a similar manner, may be equally toxic.

Whatever the source of the chemicals, many stands of forest are damaged. The toxic rains do not only affect leaves. Once absorbed by the soil, the poisons damage the nutrient gathering system of the roots, weakening the entire tree. Although many species are vulnerable, the impact of acid rain on sugar maples has caused special alarm. Woodlots in Quebec and Ontario report tree losses of 30 percent. Although much is still to be learned, the future is ominous, considering the European experience. One-half of Germany's forests are dead or terminally sick. And as trees continue to disappear, there is no consensus on a solution.

SNOWFLAKES OSCILLATE earthward. They fall on a black bear, fracturing delicate facets in landing. But the cold air and the fur protect them from the bear's body heat, and they sit up on the guard hairs, exhibiting their geometry. The bear sweeps leaf trash away from a fallen sugar maple. The leaves are brown, the bright colors of the previous week now spent.

The bear splashes more leaves aside, its back now covered with snow. The woodlands, stripped clean except for the tawny leaves of the understory beeches, recede into the haze of snowflakes. The bear withdraws too, crawling into the tunnel of a fallen tree. It puts nose to tail and settles into the long night of winter, cached in the bowels of the forest, insulated by leaves and snow, dreaming of the honeycombs it raided. The bear and the trees sleep, wrapped in each other, waiting for another spring.

Lynx.

THE NORTHERN forests region is the largest in North America. It stretches from the Atlantic Ocean to Alaska. The trees here are adapted to cold temperatures, low precipitation, and a short growing season. There are few species, with black and white spruces forming the dominant tree cover. The northern margins of the region are interspersed with tundra. Here the climate is too extreme for normal tree growth and the spruces, willows, and birch occur in dwarfed form. Beyond the last line of trees, a boundary often ill-defined and meandering, the vegetation is given over to ground-hugging grasses, herbs, mosses, lichens, and shrubs.

Tundra with dwarf willow, birch, and scattered spruces, Ogilvie Mountains, Yukon Territory.

White and black spruces, Yukon Territory.

THE OBVIOUS FEATURE of the black spruce is its club-shaped crown, quite unlike the pyramid crown of the larger white spruce. Also known as bog spruce and swamp spruce, it invariably grows on the periphery of the ubiquitous northern bogs where it is often a stunted, slow-growing tree, only adding an inch or two to its diameter in a century. In the far north, its needles are greatly reduced in length and the cones are about half their normal size. Black spruce, in addition to normal seeding, is able to reproduce by growing roots on its lower branches that eventually become new trees.

Raven over boreal forest, near Fort McMurray, Alberta.

THE BOREAL REGION of the northern forest is covered by a thick mantle of conifers mixed with birches and poplars. Most abundant are black and white spruce which are adapted to the short growing season and long winters. The range of both species extends from Newfoundland to Alaska. They tolerate a variety of soils and climates, including the great tracts of muskeg that characterize the boreal region.

Late autumn along Texas Gap Trail, Green Mountain National Forest, Vermont.

Choke cherry leaves near Ottawa, Ontario.

Willow leaves near Canmore, Alberta.

First snow on sugar maples and American beeches, Gatineau Park, Quebec.

*T*HE BEECH-MAPLE *forest is
the most prevalent deciduous
association in the transitional northern
forests. Although common throughout
the Great Lakes-St. Lawrence region,
its center of abundance is found farther
south in New England. Aside from
beauty and stature, these two species
provide essential food for many animals.
The small, triangular beechnuts are
eaten by a variety of songbirds
including blue jays, titmice, and
grosbeaks. They also provide protein
and fat for black bears, porcupines,
squirrels, and chipmunks. Maple seeds,
buds, and flowers are food for
grosbeaks, finches, and chickadees as
well as grouse and quail. Squirrels and
chipmunks store the seeds, after
removing the hull and wings, in winter
caches where they can be eaten at
leisure during the cold months.*

THROUGHOUT THE year,
members of the deer family
browse on trees and shrubs. Moose strip
off fresh spring foliage with a sideways
sweep of the head. During the summer,
they temporarily abandon the forest to
feed on the leaves and tubers of water
lilies, as well as tender new grasses. In
winter, they feed on willow, birch, and
aspen twigs, breaking them off with an
upward shrug. Moose require at least
30-40 pounds (14-18 kilograms) of
browse each day. On restricted winter
ranges, they may compete fiercely with
deer for limited food supplies.

Moose.

A FINGER OF *mixed forest
extends from the Canadian border
southward as far as North Carolina.
It follows the Appalachian mountain
chain, where elevations up to 6,600 feet
(2,000 meters) create cool temperatures
that favor the growth of conifers.
Northern species such as eastern hemlock, balsam fir, spruce, and aspen
crowd high ridges overlooking broad
valleys where pawpaw, tuliptree,
Kentucky coffeetree, magnolias, and
other southern associates grow.*

Red squirrel.

Mixed deciduous and coniferous forest, Hornbuckle Valley, North Carolina.

Sugar maples, Lincoln Gap, Green Mountain National Forest, Vermont.

*I*N ITS NORTHERN *range, sugar
maple tends to grow in pure stands.
Whole mountainsides are painted with
its orange and yellow hues in the fall.
The sap of sugar maple or the closely
related black maple is boiled down to
produce maple syrup. Red maple,
another common eastern maple, is a
smaller species that often grows in
groups. It is the most brilliant of all
maples, its rich pigments deriving from
the high concentration of sugar in its
leaves during autumn.*

Pied-billed grebe.

Common tern.

Acadian Forest, Kouchoubouguac National Park, New Brunswick.

ALTHOUGH CLOSELY related to the mixed forests of the Great Lakes-St. Lawrence River region, the Acadian forest reaches into Canada's maritime provinces and south into Maine and New England. It is distinguished most readily by the presence of red spruce, a species that grows on soils intermediate between bogs and uplands. Occasionally it forms pure stands, but it is usually found with white spruce, eastern white pine, balsam fir, eastern hemlock, yellow birch, and sugar maple. Red spruce's common name refers to the color of its flowers, cones, and bark. Bright pollen-bearing flowers appear in April and May along with reddish green cones. The trunk has reddish brown, scaly bark.

Red maple and American beech leaves among hayscented ferns and hemlock saplings, Robert Frost Memorial Trail, Vermont.

ON THE FOREST *floor, eastern
hemlock saplings sprout through
hayscented ferns and red maple leaves.
They are able to grow in the shade
of the parent trees, unlike many
species that cannot tolerate low-light
conditions. This characteristic allows
hemlocks to persist for hundreds
of years until fire or logging opens up
the forest understory. Then such areas
are colonized by fast-growing, sun-
loving species such as birch and aspen.
Eventually, through the process of
forest succession, these pioneering
species are replaced once again by
climax trees such as the hemlock.*

The atmosphere is not a perfume,
it has no taste of the distillation,
it is odorless,
It is for my mouth forever, I am in love with it,
I will go to the bank by the wood and become undisguised
and naked,
I am mad for it to be in contact with me.

WALT WHITMAN
from *Leaves of Grass*

Eastern Forests

Eastern Forests

THE SNAIL WORKS its way across the fallen hickory leaf. Nearing the edge, its shifting weight tips the leaf, allowing the transfer of body and shell onto the broad cap of a mushroom. The snail travels on a cushion of its own mucus, propelled by the rippling muscles of a large foot. A burred tongue rasps off plant cells along the way. Each day it feeds on the litter of the forest floor, cruising over leaf and mushroom, fern frond and pine cone.

Suddenly there is a rustling of leaves and then a shrill, twittering squeal — the cry of a hunting shrew. The snail is jerked into the air, its body disappearing into the shell, swinging and bumping against the interior walls. The rustling ends as the snail is pulled into the darkness.

Ragged teeth latched to the shell of its victim, the shrew races through a tunnel. Led by memory and a trail of its own pungent scent, it follows a maze of runways, most of them dug by voles, until reaching a chamber where it dumps its prey onto a pile of other snails. They are alive but sickened by the shrew's poisonous saliva.

Later in the day the shrew returns to feed on a snail. Then it takes the empty shell to the surface where a growing midden lies beneath loose layers of oak, hickory, yellow birch, and a half dozen other types of leaves. This rotting litter feeds insects, worms, sowbugs, snails, and centipedes — millions of them in a single acre. All are in turn food for the short-tailed shrew, a tiny carnivore that inhabits North America's eastern deciduous forests.

Composed primarily of broad-leaved trees, these woodlands are like no other. The diversity of species is five times greater than that found in European forests. Unlike the tropical forests to the south or the coniferous forests to the north, the appearance of these forests changes dramatically with each season. In winter the trees are stripped of leaves; in spring they are festooned with opening buds, blossoms, and catkins. Summer is the period of steady green growth; autumn brings a climax of color unparalleled elsewhere.

The deciduous forests emerge gradually from the mixed coniferous/deciduous forests to the north. They spread out from the lower slopes of the Appalachian Mountains eastward to the Atlantic Coast and westward for 600 miles (960 kilometers), here ending in forested bottomland that projects in thick fingers a further 200 miles (320 kilometers)

into Nebraska, Kansas, and Oklahoma. Another immense arm swings southward, skirting the pine forests of the coastal lowlands and reaching deep into central Texas. In all, the eastern hardwood forests touch 30 states and the province of Ontario.

Fertile soil, pushed south during the last ice age and subsequently enriched by the yearly shedding of leaves and the accumulation of other plant matter from the forests themselves, created land too fertile to be left unplowed by the settlers of these regions. The trees paid the price. Of the original forest cover which greeted the first colonists, only one-half of one percent remains today. Some of the area, however, has since been replanted or reclaimed by natural seeding. In particular, about 60 percent of the forests of New England and New York have regrown, the land unprofitable for agriculture.

The re-emergence of a forest takes place in stages, with one group of plants succeeding another until the forest community again achieves harmony with the land and its seasons. When a farmer abandons his cultivated fields, the first plants to move onto the bare soil are weeds and grasses. Their seeds are blown onto the fields by the millions, and within a couple of months the land is covered by Queen Anne's lace, tickseed, hawk-weed, and daisies, later to be joined by goldenrod, mullein, milkweed, and others. Bright sunlight inhibits tree seedlings as most are accustomed to growing in the shade. But here and there, a sprig of sassafras, white pine, or red cedar and a slip of birch, poplar, or wild cherry springs up.

Gradually the meadow is filled with small trees and shrubs, shading out the grasses and weeds. Birds and squirrels, drawn to the shelter of the pines, spread seeds from other trees in their droppings. The pines grow quickly, and their graceful limbs provide enough shade for seedlings, intolerant of sun, to gain a first foothold in the meadow. This infiltration of oaks, maples, tulip-trees, and others is the beginning of the end for the pines, although they will likely dominate the forest for another century.

With the passing years, the canopy thickens as the leaves of birches and cherries are added to those of the white pines. Now the understory is too dark for the seedlings of these species to germinate. Fires, storms, insect infestations, and diseases claim one pine after another. With each loss, the slow-growing seedlings of oak and maple stretch their limbs into the opening, eventually claiming the space as their own. In this way the pioneering trees are replaced, or succeeded, by climax species. These trees, which produce seedlings capable of growing in the shade, will achieve permanent dominance of the forest as long as it stands.

The eastern forests are of varied composition. In the northern regions — southern Ontario, northern Indiana and Ohio, and western Pennsylvania — the canopy is made up almost exclusively of beech and sugar maple with white oak and tuliptree occuring occasionally. To the west, the forests of north-western Illinois, southwestern Wisconsin, and southern Minnesota are dominated by sugar maple and basswood. The understory of both these associations is composed primarily of the saplings of the dominant species. The forest floor is spread with shrubs — often elderberry, a variety of ferns, and wildflowers such as jack-in-the-pulpit, wild ginger, and hepatica.

In the far southwestern portions of the deciduous forest zone, precipitation diminishes and the Ozark Highlands of Oklahoma, Arkansas, and Missouri are dominated by oak-hickory climax. Nevertheless, there is much floral diversity due to varied topography and soils, and the incursion of species from surrounding forest associations. Low rainfall is chief among the factors which create a relatively open understory typified by the presence of flowering dogwood and blueberries.

In the remaining south and central portions of the deciduous zone, the number of species increases, and the forests are distinguished by a varied, undifferentiated climax community rather than by the dominance of a particular association. Here, sycamore, buckeye, sassafras, black cherry, magnolia, basswood, tuliptree, and sweet gum invade the stands of oaks, hickories, and maples. A single lush valley may harbor more than 70 species. Pines, too, become more varied as you move south.

The white pines of New England are replaced by pitch and Virginia pines in the central part of the zone; loblolly, longleaf, and slash pines are found in the southern reaches.

Dramatic examples of these hardwood forests occur in lowland areas of Great Smoky Mountains National Park in Tennessee and North Carolina. The mild temperatures and heavy precipitation spread mists and fog through the mountains, giving them their name and creating a climate ideal for forest growth. In the coves (low-lying pockets of land surrounded by mountains) and valley bottoms, rainfall reaches 100 inches (2.5 meters) per year. These areas shelter the most extensive tracts of primeval deciduous forest in North America. In addition, 15 species reach record size, making these forests the most lush of any temperate region in the world, except for the Pacific Coast. Cucumber trees, yellow buckeyes, and eastern hemlocks develop trunks 6 feet (1.8 meters) in diameter; the largest is a tuliptree which measures more than 7.5 feet (2.3 meters) across.

Though these forests may impress with their extraordinary dimensions, of equal fascination are the wildflowers that emerge in May. They spread their petals under the spring sun, hoping to attract a pollinating bee or butterfly before the trees above leaf out and shut off the light. Trillium, spring beauty, trout lily, bloodroot, honeysuckle, and hundreds more species spatter color over the woodland, small ephemeral sculptings turned out amidst the permanent array of ferns (maidenhair, rattlesnake, and interrupted) and mosses. Above the herbaceous layer on the forest floor are elderberry, laurel, rhododendron, dogwood, serviceberry, and other flowering shrubs and trees, which add their own accents of color to the spring season.

ITS BRANCHES extend at right angles from the trunk, projecting over the blue beeches, high-bush cranberries, and sassafras below. The longest days of the year have put an end to the buzzy notes of the blackburnian warblers that plied its upper-most limbs. The leaves turn with the sun as it arcs over them, absorbing energy to manufacture wood for the trunk, to send its great tap root deeper, its new branches higher into the canopy. But now this white oak is more intent on producing acorns — emissaries that will carry its genes into the forests of the future. For the tree they are a link with eternity.

Normally, a few thousand acorns are dropped by the oak during the autumn, but this is a mast year, one of unusual abundance, and the oak will litter the forest floor with more than 15,000 nuts. Still green, they cling to the twigs, safe, it would seem, from the scores of bird and mammal species that wait for them to ripen and fall. But acorn weevils have already visited nearly a thousand of them, boring through the soft shell with long snouts, depositing eggs inside the nut. In two months, when the acorns have dropped to the forest floor, the larvae will emerge, having consumed most of the inner tissue. Meanwhile, different beetles have chewed open a few hundred others, and of these, some have become infested with fly larvae, 40 or 50 to an acorn. They attract scavengers — mites, springtails, more beetles. The acorn's interior becomes host to animals eating and being eaten, an organic stew that in turn is invaded with bacteria, algae, and fungi.

Despite these losses, the autumn season is a bountiful one for the wood ducks, wild turkeys, and squirrels that feed under the spreading limbs of the oak by day, and for the white-footed mice, black bears, deer, and raccoons that forage here after dark. The feast will last for several weeks. Gradually the hoard of nuts will disappear, most into the stomachs of birds and mammals. Some, flawed by nature or attacked by insects while still growing, will lie derelict among the leaves, meat eaten, empty shells becoming home for ants and centipedes. The healthy acorns, however, began germinating as soon as they fell, their delicate roots probing the soft humus, seeking to anchor themselves to the earth, working against the odds that they will produce acorns of their own. Fewer than one in a hundred will sprout, and of these, half will die.

Although its method of reproduction may seem inefficient, the white oak nevertheless thrives throughout the eastern hardwood forest region. It does not rival the sycamore in girth, nor the tuliptree in height, but its trunk attains diameters of 6 feet (1.8 meters) and its uppermost branches may reach 100 feet (30 meters) into the canopy. Distinctly impressive is its crown, with a record span of 150 feet (46 meters) for a specimen growing in the open, and its age, which for the oldest trees is estimated at eight centuries.

Of North America's trees, the acorns of the white oak are unsurpassed as wildlife food. Combined with the fruits of other oaks, they feed more than 100 species of birds and mammals. Other deciduous trees are also valuable sources of food. Walnuts and hickory nuts are important to squirrels, mice, and chipmunks, which can gnaw through the tough outer shells. These rodents also feed on beech nuts, as do birds able to penetrate the thinner shells. Black cherry and pin cherry trees produce fleshy fruits gorged by songbirds in late summer and fall.

As a wildlife food source, the pines are next in importance to the oaks. Their seeds are pulled from the cones by bobwhite, mourning doves, songbirds, cottontails, mice, and chipmunks. The foliage and twigs are browsed by white-tailed deer. In all, more than 80 species feed on them. A hundred years ago, the chestnut tree was one of the most important food resources for many forest animals. Today it is little more than a memory.

A WARM UPWELLING breeze carries the microscopic spores for miles before the day cools and they settle onto the forest. There are millions of them, and by chance a few fall into the borings of a wood beetle, making their way through the bark of a chestnut tree and into the cambium layer. The tree is 10 stories high; its crown spreads over the slope, waving slender catkins. Along with several hundred other chestnuts, it began growing on this hillside two centuries earlier. Within a few years, the tiny spores will kill every one of them.

In 1904, a fungus was discovered on a chestnut tree in the New York Zoological Park. The fungus is believed to have come to America from the Orient on a shipment of lumber. It spread rapidly on wind-borne spores. By the mid 1930s, nearly every tree on the continent was fatally infected. Thousands were felled by chain saws in order to stop the spread of the disease, but to no avail. From Maine to Alabama their skeletons loomed from the forests, twisted remnants of a species nearly dead.

The slowly decaying hulks stood for decades. Today most have fallen — pushed over by a storm, or simply by time and gravity. Once prone on the forest floor, the trunks were splintered by woodpeckers and ripped apart by black bears searching for grubs. Chunks of limb were softened by termites, the fibers shredded by the slender fingers of fungi and the cells consumed by bacteria.

Strangled and broken by a foreign disease, the chestnut crumbled, slumped, and dissolved into the earth and perhaps into history. As scientists still struggle to find a way to defeat the blight, a natural strain of the fungus has appeared which is not fatal. Should it spread, supplanting the deadly strains, chestnut trees might once again fill our woodlands. But nature's designs are played out like a sunrise — with surprise and certainty. Only time can reveal the fate of declining species, such as the chestnut, or that of proliferating ones, such as man.

Portfolio
Eastern Forests

Wood duck preening.

THE EASTERN forests are composed of broad-leaved trees, primarily maples, oaks, beech, and hickories. To survive winter cold, dryness, and reduced light conditions, broad-leaved trees enter a state of dormancy. This is initiated by the dramatic change in color of the leaves, which are subsequently shed to prevent the loss of water during winter through transpiration. In spring, when the soil grows full of water from the snowmelt, sap surges from the roots, the buds open and spread their leaves, and photosynthesis resumes for another season.

Leaves of white oak, sugar maple, American sycamore, eastern redbud, and tuliptree, Aullwood Aububon Sanctuary, Ohio.

Northern red oak and American beech, Pisgah National Forest, North Carolina.

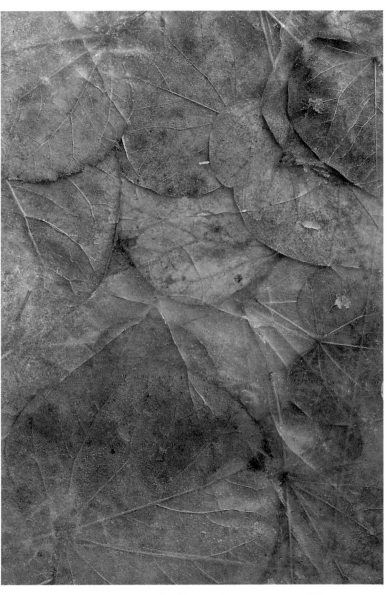

Eastern redbud leaves along Whitewater River, Indiana.

EVERY AUTUMN billions of leaves fall onto the forest floor. At first they join the litter of whole leaves and leaf fragments that form the uppermost layer of the soil. As each leaf is buried, bacteria and fungi feed on it, breaking it down and causing it to decay. The rotting process releases minerals that are absorbed by other plants. Each species of leaf decays at a different rate. Maple leaves decompose quickly, beech leaves slowly. As the leaves crumble and disintegrate, they become part of the top layer of the soil known as humus, a nutrient-rich substance which is vital to forest growth.

Yellow birch, American beech, and striped maple, Virginia.

Black ash and celandine meadow, Turkey Point, Ontario.

Raccoon.

COMMON IN the eastern forests, raccoons are found near watercourses where they hunt crayfish, frogs, small fish, and turtles. They are seldom active before dark, spending most of the day snoozing in their den or in the crotch of a tree. Raccoons are agile climbers and their dens are often located in hollow trees, particularly maples, elms, and basswoods. Dens are situated at least 10 feet (3 meters) above the ground and are lined with leaves. Raccoons may also occupy hollow logs, caves, overturned stumps, burrows excavated by other mammals, and deserted nests of hawks and crows.

A TREE'S BARK *is its skin. The inner layer, called the cambium, contains millions of living cells that are constantly dividing and producing new wood that pushes the previous year's bark outward. The oldest bark forms the tough exterior layer which protects the tree from insects, fungi, and fire damage. Bark varies in thickness. Sequoia bark can be more than a foot (30 centimeters) thick and is a significant factor in reducing damage from forest fires. Bark texture varies with the age of a tree. Some trees, such as the tuliptree, have smooth young bark that cracks and fissures into deeper furrows as the trees age. Others, such as American sycamore and shagbark hickory, develop bark that sloughs off as the tree matures.*

Black cherry bark, Richmond, Indiana.

American sycamore bark, Fairhaven, Ohio.

Deciduous forest, Allegheny Plateau, Pennsylvania.

AUTUMN'S WARM *hues in the eastern forests cover thousands of square miles. The dominant color of any particular area usually results from only a few species. Red oaks, maples, wild cherries, sumac, sweetgum, and dogwood provide the most brilliant reds. Birches, tuliptrees, hickories, ashes, and sycamores paint the hillsides yellow. Climate affects the intensity of color from year to year. Peak color in central Canada and New England occurs during the last week of September and the first two weeks of October, while farther south in the Great Smoky Mountains, the last week of October is prime time.*

*T*HE CLIMATE *and rugged land of the Great Smoky Mountains of Tennessee and North Carolina create a wide range of growing conditions. As a result over 100 species of trees are found in this relatively small area. On the highest peaks northern evergreens such as red spruce and Fraser fir dominate. Along moist, shady slopes are eastern hemlocks, while pines and oaks cover the dry and exposed ridges. In the coves and river valleys at mid-to-low elevations, eastern hardwood species thrive. Here the rich soils, mild temperatures, and abundant rainfall foster the growth of huge deciduous trees, with nearly 20 species approaching record size.*

Canada geese over Great Smoky Mountains.

TULIPTREES, ALSO called yellow poplars, are among the tallest trees in the eastern forests. Their straight trunks measure 8-10 feet (2.4-3.0 meters) in diameter, and the uppermost branches can be up to 200 feet (61 meters) above the forest floor. Tuliptrees range from southern Ontario to northern Florida, sometimes forming pure stands on moist, well-drained slopes. The thin, gray bark on younger trees becomes brown, thick, and deeply furrowed with age. The leaves are distinctive in shape and turn from a glossy pale green in summer to a rich gold in fall. The tuliptree derives its name from the large, cup-shaped flowers that emerge after the leaves in spring. In Tennessee, it is still referred to as canoewood, since the Cherokee Indians carved dugouts from the trunks.

Tuliptree, black walnut, flowering dogwood, and sweetgum, Great Smoky Mountains National Park, North Carolina.

*T*HE GREAT BLUE HERON is
the best-known and most widely
distributed of all North American
herons. More than 3 feet (1 meter) tall,
with a wingspan twice its height, it is a
majestic bird whether poised rock-still
or flying to a tree top perch, broad
wings pumping in slow motion and
reed-like legs trailing behind. Although
adapted for feeding in shallow waters,
the great blue is also at home in the
trees, where it builds its large nest of
woven branches and twigs.

Great blue heron.

Young great horned owl.

*O*AKS ARE common in the eastern forests. Northern species are deciduous, while many southern species are evergreen. The genus can be divided into two groups: the white oaks have leaves with rounded lobes or regular toothed margins, and the red oaks have leaves with spine-tipped or bristle-tipped lobes. The fruit of the oak is the acorn, a thin-shelled nut seated in cup of tightly overlapping scales. Acorns, especially those of white oaks, are a food staple for many kinds of wildlife. In the autumn, squirrels hide acorns in the loose surface soil of the forest floor to be eaten later in the winter. Many of these acorns germinate, a small percentage eventually grow into acorn producing trees, ensuring food supplies for future generations of squirrels.

Northern red oak and sugar and red maples, Nantahala National Forest, North Carolina.

Beech leaves near Ithaca, New York.

Eastern flowering dogwood leaves near Port Rowan, Ontario.

The blossoms of the
jessamine, ever pleasing, lay
steeped in dew, the humming
bee was collecting her winter's
store from the snowy flowers
of the native orange; and the
little warblers frisked along the
twigs of the smilax. Now, amid
the tall pines of the forest, the
sun's rays began to force their
ways, and as the dense mists
dissolved in the atmosphere,
the bright luminary at length
shone through.

JOHN JAMES AUDUBON
from *Audubon and His Journals*

Southern Forests

Southern Forests

A DOZEN WOOD ducklings rest in the cavity of the bald cypress; a fuzzy, brown pile that you could cup in two hands. They gather strength with each passing minute.

Pee-ee, pee-ee, pee-ee. Their mother's voice is low and pleading. The brood squirms at the sound, and one duckling takes a first step, tiny claws hooking into the wood. The calls of the mother add strength to its efforts. It takes a second step toward the entrance three feet above, and a third, and behind it the pile of down begins to unravel as one duckling after another follows. They creep up the trunk's interior to get their first glimpse of the South Carolina swamp that is their home.

Out in the forest, the mother grows more excited. She calls and circles, weaving through the tightly knit canopy of baldcypress, water tupelo, sweetgum, and loblolly pine. The wood duck nest is 60 feet (18 meters) above the waters of the swamp.

The ducklings begin to appear in the tree cavity's

entrance, filling the threshold. Still the brood pushes from below, drawn to the parent's call. Whether pressured by its nest mates or coaxed by the cooing of the hen now swimming in the water, one duckling takes to the air.

It descends without commotion, stumpy wings working against the atmosphere, tiny webs paddling. The egg-shaped body tilts and twists, plummeting out of control to plop into the water. Twelve plops, twelve sets of concentric ripples spreading across the pool, broken by the knees and buttresses of baldcypress, until the energy is spent somewhere beyond, in the deepest confines of the swamp, in the dark privacy of the bobcat and the alligator.

By late afternoon the ducklings are huddled with their mother near a dwarf palmetto, exhausted from the excitement of the swamp. They are asleep, warmed by sunlight penetrating the meshes of Spanish moss, soothed by the sounds of the forest. The calls of the barred owl drift by, pushing through the close understory of holly, yaupon, pawpaw, and ironwood for nearly a mile. The *kuk-kuk-kuk-kuk-kuk* of the pileated woodpecker slashes through the loose vines and hanging epiphytes. Opening its wings in short bursts, swoop-gliding high in the canopy, it calls while in flight, a song that shakes the olive green precincts of the forest. There are other sounds: the grunt of an alligator, the hiss of an oppossum, the crackle of leaves beneath a deer, the whine of a cicada. But as with most woodland recitals, the notes are widely spaced, sometimes minutes apart.

This forest at Congaree Swamp in South Carolina is made up of large trees — baldcypress, sweetgum, water tupelo, oaks, and others growing out of brown water. The understory is hung with wild grape vines, trumpet creepers, poison ivy, and yellow jessamine, and thick with smaller trees such as holly, ironwood, and dogwood. It is typical of the virgin swamplands found throughout the southern lowland region, a vast area of many different forests. In addition to the swamps of the floodplains, there are upland forests dominated by pines. Between these two extremes are hardwood forests and mixed stands of conifers and broad-leaved species.

Wherever one travels in the southern coastal lowlands, pine trees are not far away. Pines link the many diverse tree associations that are found here. The pine lands, as these forests are commonly called, occupy southeastern Maryland and Virginia, most of North Carolina, South Carolina, Arkansas, and Georgia, Louisiana, Mississippi, Florida, and eastern portions of Texas and Oklahoma. They are bounded on the east by the Atlantic Ocean and on the south by the Gulf of Mexico. To the north, as the soils grow more fertile and the elevation increases, they merge gradually with the deciduous forests. To the west they thin out, generally giving way to oaks which in turn surrender to the diminished rainfall of the prairie grasslands.

Within these boundaries, there may be pure stands

of pines — longleaf, shortleaf, slash, and loblolly being the principal species. But as a rule, the pines are well mixed with oaks, hickories, magnolias, sweetgums, ashes, and scores of other species; the mixture is dependent on local growing conditions. Different pine species dominate certain habitats: sand pines on sterile soils, loblolly pines in low-lying areas, and slash pines in subtropical regions. In the southern half of Florida, the forests are generally composed of broad-leaved tropical species, typical to islands of the West Indies. Although different in species composition, the forests of the Rio Grande Valley of Texas similarly exhibit tropical influences.

The forests of the southern lowlands, like those anywhere, are a product of soil and climate. Here both factors favor the growth of pines. Unlike the soils of the eastern hardwood forests, which are rich in humus, a material that holds water like a sponge, these soils are comprised mostly of porous sand and gravel. Although rainfall is ample, more than 50 inches (1.3 meters) per year, it is held in the soil only briefly so that trees cannot make full use of it. Consequently, trees that grow here must be adapted to aridity. Pines have thin, waxy needles which, compared with broad-leaved trees, have less surface area and thus lose less water through transpiration.

Another climatic influence on the pine lands is the occurrence of intense electrical storms, especially during the summer. The lightning causes many forest fires each year. Pines have thick, insulating bark, and few of them are killed. In addition, where the trees are needle-leaved rather than broad-leaved, there is less accumulation of debris on the forest floor. As a result, fires sweep through quickly without intense heat build-up.

Although the pine-dominated forests burn regularly, they are basically immune to serious damage by fire. Hurricanes can be a greater threat. High winds can topple swaths of forests, leaving only young and supple trees undamaged. Water driven from the ocean sweeps up logs and other debris which batter individual trees. Saplings and understory species may be uprooted or buried in gravel and silt. Once the winds have calmed and the floods have receded, the forest begins to repair itself, but it takes decades, even centuries, for the effects of severe storms to disappear.

The continuity of these pine-dominated woodlands, sweeping from the Atlantic Coast across the southern United States into Texas and Oklahoma, is interrupted along the lower Mississippi River basin. Here repeated and prolonged flooding of the lowlands limits the growth of pines, although they are still present on elevated sites. The bayous are lined with the usual complement of water tupelo and in the more remote reaches, large baldcypress. In addition, waterlocust, water hickory, and sometimes planertree, are common. The deposition of silt left by receding waters creates rich soils which favor many hardwood species typically found in the deciduous forests to the north. On well-drained land tuliptrees, sycamores, oaks, ashes, maples, and elms thrive. Acorns, pecans, and persimmons are heavy on the trees in autumn, feeding all manner of creatures from white-footed mice and Carolina chickadees to wild turkeys and red foxes.

Human industry has destroyed nearly all the virgin forests of the southern lowland region, including the wildlife they sustained. The few virgin forest stands that remain are mostly protected in government or private sanctuaries: Congaree Swamp in South Carolina, Okefenokee Swamp in Georgia, Corkscrew Swamp and Big Cypress National Preserve in Florida, Big Thicket National Preserve in Texas, and others.

THEY RETURN SINGLY, one ghostly form after another stealing through the mist, white ibises and great egrets assembling in a stand of sweetgum and loblolly pine to preen and then sleep out the night. The trees are filled with birds, discernible only as a hundred or so ghostly forms. The pine woods treefrogs high above them are invisible. Even in daylight at close range, their mottled skin hides them against the loblolly branches. To the birds below they are only sounds signaling all is well: a chorus of mellow tapping, like drumsticks struck one against another. The tiny frogs call into the darkness. Their sounds organize the

mating strategies of the group: tapping, retapping, overtapping, a plethora of notes piling up, bumping together, a confusion of timing that backs into itself, until the melody emerges, abstract and soothing, fusing with the moonlight and the humid air.

Until the end of the Civil War, egrets and wild turkeys, copperheads and cottonmouths, and probably even jaguars and ocelots lived unmolested among the pines, oaks, beeches, and magnolias of East Texas. This was a region of tangled jungle, pine savannas, cypress swamps, and unbreachable canebrakes. The climax forests grew immense trees with loblolly pine, beech, and magnolia forming a canopy over maples and oaks. Sandy hilltops were covered with longleaf pine, bluejack oak, and tree sparkleberry. The mild climate, abundant rainfall, and varied soils produced great botanical diversity. It was a biological crossroads where southern swamplands met the eastern hardwood forests and the desert flora of the Southwest.

The Big Thicket, as it came to be called, remained relatively undisturbed until the end of the last century. The dense forests and low-lying lands, often flooded, turned back the waves of settlers that had washed over most other parts of North America decades earlier. But with the discovery of oil, the wilderness could no longer withstand the pressures of civilization. Railroads were laid through the forests; spur lines were sent out just long enough to cut and cart off the timber. Roads were built and wells drilled. A devastating hurricane and an outbreak of pine beetles caused further damage to the forests. The influx of immigrants removed more trees to make room for farms, housing developments, and industries. Today the Big Thicket is small and broken up. Two or three percent of its original 3,500,000 acres remain protected in a handful of scattered tracts north of Beaumont, Texas.

THE SOUTHERNMOST reaches of the coastal lowland extend to the tip of the Florida peninsula and beyond into the Keys. Here climate is moderated by the Gulf of Mexico and the Atlantic Ocean. Temperatures range between 60 and 90 degrees Fahrenheit (15 and 32 degrees Celsius) year-round, even at night, providing for an unending growing season and the emergence of tropical vegetation. During any month there are plants in flower or fruit.

Although the climate is unique, in other ways this area differs little from the rest of the coastal lowland. The topography is flat. Soils are thin and lain over sand, gravel, or limestone, materials which allow rain to drain quickly into the water table. Although yearly precipitation is ample, it falls mainly during the summer, leaving long periods when plants must go without water. Together, these factors create near desert conditions, and many areas harbor plants such as prickly pear and mesquite, which you would expect to see in Arizona.

For millions of years, fire has prevented much of the coastal lowland forest from reaching climax, and varied stages of subclimax development are evidenced throughout the zone. Certain conditions, however, pre-empt the effects of fire and allow the development of communities in which the species composition achieves stasis. Limestone ridges are usually covered with slash pine and saw-palmetto, the former is protected by its layered, insulating bark, the latter by keeping its roots in limestone pockets where fire cannot reach. The sea protects the coastal fringe of mangrove forests, perched atop stiff, stiltlike roots projecting from the salt water. Similarly, water protects the baldcypress swamps and other submerged hardwood communities along rivers.

Islands of land (hammocks) raised above the surrounding floodplain are protected at least part of the time from wildfires by the water barrier. When this situation is permanent, climax development of dry tropical forest occurs. Hammocks are common in the Everglades, and they stand out as islands in the sea of sawgrass. Some are not much bigger than a backyard, others may occupy square miles. The names of many trees suggest their tropical nature: cocoplum, strangler fig, paradise-tree, gumbo-limbo, papaya, tamarind, royal palm.

Typical of tropical forests, the climax community is not dominated by a single group of trees, but instead 60 or 70 species may share the canopy in a single hammock. Trunks and limbs are decorated with air plants — Spanish moss, resurrection fern, orchids, and bromeliads. Vines and lianas hang from the highest limbs. Except for the color, such forests are everyone's idea of a jungle. But the high intensity of sunlight and periodic droughts reduce the forest's production of chlorophyl, and the green is faded, the vegetation often shriveled and brittle.

THE SHADOWS move like lasers over the terrain. Even from ground level you can enjoy their mathematical certainty. They trace the flight paths of the birds above. Shadows arc over the pond, unbroken until they reach the hammock; they twitch upward and shoot raggedly through the royal palms and mahoganies, then across the expanse of sawgrass, humping over the hedge of mangroves and swooping out onto the bay.

One shadow loops smoothly back toward shore. It grows smaller and more distinct, and fuses with a black vulture that lands with much commotion. Its weight pushes the tips of a mangrove into the water, launching other vultures that had come before, separating them again into birds and shadows.

The mangroves are heavy with vultures. By turns they descend the latticework of roots to water level where a Key deer is entangled, its bloated carcass heaving with the incoming swells. It is difficult for the vultures to probe the interior of the body and at the same time maintain their precarious footing. Periodically, one slips off and struggles to shore, half flying, half swimming, where it stands on the beach with wings spread to catch the sun.

The Key deer lives on the twigs, foliage, and acorns of the forest. Aside from vultures, its decomposing body will nourish fish, turtles, and invertebrates. In turn, these animals will be eaten by herons and eagles, which will release their droppings from nests and roosts onto the forest floor. These nutrients will be taken up by the plants on which the Key deer feeds, completing a cycle as delicate and essential as a cast shadow.

127

Alligator.

Loblolly pine, black willow, southern red oak, and cedar elm, Big Thicket National Preserve, Texas.

*U*NLIKE THE FORESTS to
the north, which are dominated
by two or three tree species, many
climax forests of the south consist of
an even mixture of 10 or more species,
including pine, oak, and hickory as well
as tuliptree, sycamore, and others. This
undifferentiated community is typical of
tropical forests, where the variety of
plant species is much greater than in
temperate regions.

Baldcypress swamp, Congaree Swamp, South Carolina.

Limpkin.

Snowy egret.

*T*HE TREES OF *swamps provide ideal roosting and nesting sites for birds. The surrounding waters minimize human access and provide good habitat for animals that birds prey upon. Large wading birds, such as egrets, herons, ibises, spoonbills, and wood storks, are colonial nesters. Hundreds, and sometimes even thousands, of pairs take up residence in a stand of baldcypress. Individual*

trees may contain 10 or more nests. Although living in colonies creates competition for food and nesting sites, the greater density of individuals provides an advantage in discouraging predators, especially from raiding nests in the core of the colony. In addition, since breeding birds lay their eggs at about the same time, there are so many young that predators simply cannot eat them all.

MANGROVE SWAMPS are found in tropical areas at the edge of the sea. They form coastal barriers, receiving the brunt of storms and hurricanes, thereby protecting the shoreline. The mangroves' stiltlike roots project into the water and slowly extend the shoreline by trapping silt, sand, and other debris carried in by waves and tides. This semiaquatic existence has produced interesting botanical adaptations. The mangrove's umbrella-shaped crown is formed of evergreen leaves that exude salt on their undersurfaces. Mangrove seeds germinate on the parent tree, and when the seedlings drop off, they float until contacting land where they start to grow immediately.

Yellow-crowned night herons and mangroves, Texas coast.

*E*IGHT SPECIES OF *pine tree grow in the southern coastal lowlands. The principal ones are shortleaf, longleaf, and loblolly pine. They can be easily distinguished by their needles and cones. Longleaf pine, as the name suggests, has the longest needles (10-15 inches/ 25-38 centimeters) and largest cones (6-10 inches/15-25 centimeters), while shortleaf has the shortest needles (3-5 inches/8-13 centimeters) and smallest cones (1-2 inches/3-5 centimeters). The cones and needles of loblolly pine are of intermediate dimension. Because of their fast growth and resistance to fire and drought, pines are able to establish permanent subclimax forests in areas where hardwoods would otherwise shade them out.*

Loblolly pine, sugar maple, and sweetgum, Piedmont National Wildlife Refuge, Georgia.

White oak bark, Sam Houston National Forest, Texas.

Black oak, overcup oak, and sugarberry leaves, Big Thicket National Preserve, Texas.

Southern red oak, blackjack oak, tuliptree, sweetgum, and loblolly pine, Stone Mountain Park, Georgia.

Pileated woodpecker.

THE BASS drummer of the deep woods, the pileated woodpecker is the largest woodpecker commonly seen in North America. It chops into decaying trunks or rotted stumps for carpenter ants, wood-boring beetles, and other small invertebrates. Like other woodpeckers, the pileated has special adaptations for extracting its food from trees. Its brain is housed inside a thick skull and surrounded by a thin, shock-absorbing cushion of air. It has big neck muscles, a flint hard bill, and a long, extensible, sticky tongue tipped with barbs for snagging grubs or slurping up sap.

Green anole.

Sabal palm and saw palmetto, Myakka River State Park, Florida.

Jubliant winds and waters
sound in grand harmonious
symphonies — wild music
flowing on forever from a
thousand thousand sources,
winds in hollows of the glaciers
glinting on crystal angles, winds
on crags, in trees, among the
elastic needles sweeping soft
and low with silken rhythm, and
winds murmuring through the
grasses...

JOHN MUIR
Journal Entry on Mt. Rainier

Mountain Forests

Mountain Forests

FRONT HOOVES suspended, rear hooves locked into the thin alpine soil, eyes blank as stones, the two rams seem driven by a single brain. The curled horns accelerate toward each other. *Clonk*. The sound is tight; it lies flat against the mountainside and dies abruptly. The animals meet like a clap of the hands. Each collision comes before you are ready for it. There is no giving of ground, no loss of footing, no hot breath, no leaking saliva. After millions of years of rehearsal, the choreography is precise, and for the moment the combat is mostly ritual.

The bighorn sheep lives in and about the forests of the Rocky Mountains. The sheep and the forests have evolved as products of the rugged terrain and the harsh climate. Unable to graze in deep snow, bighorns pass the winter at low elevations, where temperatures are warmer and snowfall is lighter. Here the trees are stunted by dry conditions and scattered over rolling grasslands and sagebrush benches. As winter fades, the bighorns move up the slopes into the montane forests where there are large trees growing in open stands. It is not as warm at these higher elevations. Air masses rising against the mountainsides cool and lose some of their moisture, creating better growing conditions for plants. Like other sheep, bighorns prefer grasses and herbs, and it is not until late winter that they become hungry enough to browse here on tree needles and twigs.

As days lengthen and the snowpack shrinks, the sheep migrate higher into the subalpine forests. Here precipitation is greatest. The trees grow in dense stands. Some species develop spirelike crowns, which allow the accumulating snow and ice to slide off harmlessly. Subalpine forests are found throughout the Rocky Mountains as well as other mountain regions of the West, including the coastal ranges.

When summer arrives, the sheep have climbed into the alpine meadows. Here the trees are stunted, most no taller than a man. Forests cannot survive due to the brief growing season, drying winds, and blowing snow and ice. For a few weeks, the bighorns graze on the burgeoning grasses and herbs, chewing on paint-brushes, glacier lilies, and lupines, as lambs bleat and ramble through the flocks.

The distribution of tree species in the mountainous regions of the West is dependent on temperature, soil type, and rainfall. In general, however, elevation plays the principal role, as it affects both rainfall and temperature. And although diverse associations are

to be found throughout the region, you can usually tell how high up a mountain you have hiked by identifying the trees at hand. The forests here are less luxuriant than those found on the coast. Nevertheless, tree growth is heavy in many areas.

The vegetation of the mountain foothills comprises a transition zone between prairie or scrub desert and the stands of montane forests found at higher elevations. It is open, sun-baked terrain covered with grasses — green in spring, yellow-brown for the rest of the year — and a scattering of stunted trees: ponderosa pine and Rocky Mountain juniper in the northern areas, and pinon pine and juniper to the south.

In this habitat, animals are heard and seen easily: the fluting calls of western meadowlarks sift through the trees in the early morning, kingbirds flutter out from dead branches to snatch insects, turkey vultures tilt silently against the persistence of blue sky. In spring, ravens probe at mounds of carrion unveiled by melting snow, while magpies argue restlessly nearby. Coyotes quarter through the meadows, pausing to peer over their shoulders, hoping to see what their noses have smelled. Young foxes are flopped on the humped entrances to their dens, waiting for their parents to return with a ground squirrel or vole.

THE MONTANE FORESTS are sandwiched between the prairies and scrublands below and the subalpine forests above. They are spread over the mountainous regions of Idaho, Montana, Wyoming, Colorado, Arizona, New Mexico, and Utah, western portions of South Dakota and Alberta, and eastern British Columbia, Oregon, and Washington. The mountains here are composed of many different ranges, running generally in a north-south direction. To the west this area is bounded by the Great Basin Desert lying in the rain shadow of the coastal mountains and the Sierra Nevadas; to the east are the Great Plains, another region too dry to support forest growth. The montane forest region is interspersed, especially in the southern half, by broad deserts.

These forests exhibit varied composition depending on factors of weather, terrain, and forest fire. In general, ponderosa pine and Douglas-fir are the most prominent species through most of the mid-elevations of the Rockies, ponderosa pine claiming the lower slopes of the zone and Douglas-fir taking over above it. These uncrowded stands snake down from the slopes along coulees and streambeds to meet the savanna. In the northern Rocky Mountains, it becomes too cold for ponderosa pine, and it gives way to Douglas-fir, which in turn is supplanted by lodgepole pine in the northernmost ranges of British Columbia. On the eastern flanks of the Rockies in Montana and Alberta, cold weather again limits the growth of Douglas-fir in favor of lodgepole pine. In places the rolling hills are packed monotonously with the lodgepoles' bare, thin trunks.

The ponderosa pine sheds floppy bunches of needles and huge cones, creating a thick layer of debris that permits only a sparse understory — most often a combination of brittle mats of broken juniper and kinnikinnick. As you move upward through the montane forest, the ponderosa pines are replaced by other trees in addition to Douglas-firs, primarily western larch (in the northern Rockies), limber pine, and trembling aspen.

The trembling aspen is common in the Rockies, being most abundant in Utah and western Colorado. Its name is derived from its long-stemmed leaves, which flutter in the slightest breeze. The smooth, white trunks are marked by dark, warty patches where bark has been removed by feeding elk. Even though aspens produce abundant wind-dispersed seeds, many groves are spread by the root systems, which send up new saplings. In spring and summer, the broken canopy of the aspen groves encourages the growth of wildflowers and shrubs which cannot survive in the dense shade of conifers. The color of blooming columbines, saxifrages, Canada violets, and heaths attracts insects and hummingbirds. Bushes such as shrubby cinquefoil, buffalo berry, huckleberry, and kinnikinnick provide food and reproductive habitat for birds, deer, squirrels, and porcupines. In autumn, aspens are transformed, almost overnight, into masses of gold.

They are joined in this celebration of the season by the western larch, a conifer that goes unnoticed for the rest of the year, its fresh green foliage offering little distinction from the heavier greens of the pines, firs, and spruces with which it associates. But at the onset of frost and the decrease in summer rains, its clusters of flexible needles change into tints of yellow, bronze, and gold, for a few weeks illuminating the somber slopes before they are shed. The western larch achieves its greatest size — 6 feet (2 meters) in diameter — and abundance in Montana, but it is also found in British Columbia, Alberta, Washington, Oregon, and Idaho.

A CRACK ECHOES through the dry air; seconds later, another crack, this time accented with a final deep flourish. Through the trees in the direction of the sound, an osprey flaps heavily; from its talons hangs a twisted snag the length of a broom handle. By diving onto the tree and grasping a branch in its talons, the osprey is able to break off sticks needed to construct its lakeside nest. An Engelmann spruce, the source of this material, is long dead, decaying as it stands, until one day in late winter, laden with ice and snow, it will topple in the wind.

Meanwhile, for decades perhaps, its branches are shed for the osprey's nest, a broadening platform that grows ever safer for the clumsy young reared each year. The missing branches leave openings for insects and micro-organisms to enter the tree, accelerating the rot and creating food for three-toed woodpeckers, brown creepers, and red-breasted nuthatches. A red-shafted flicker may chisel a cavity out of the softened wood, and when its nesting is finished, the hole may be used in succession by hooded mergansers, western screech owls, kestrels, red squirrels, and flying squirrels.

Engelmann spruce is found in the subalpine forests, the community of trees which grows highest on the mountainside just below the alpine tundra. Near the Pacific Coast, these forests usually begin at about 3,000 feet (900 meters) and extend to treeline at about 7,000 feet (2,100 meters). As you move inland they are found at greater elevations, stretching from 4,000 feet (1,200 meters) to 7,500 feet (2,300 meters) in the Rocky Mountains.

The lofty terrain wrings moisture from passing weather systems, creating growths of similar-sized conifers. These forests are thicker than those found in the montane zone below, and wildlife is seen but briefly amidst the crowded trunks and limbs. Adapted to the brief summer growing season, heavy snows, and low temperatures of lingering winter, the trees mantle the tops of mountains, and in places their thin, ice-shedding spires climb near-vertical slopes. The Douglas-firs of lower elevations become less prominent, and new species are encountered. Engelmann spruce is the characteristic tree of high mountain slopes from British Columbia to Arizona and New Mexico. It grows in mixed forests with white fir, limber pine, lodgepole pine, mountain hemlock, subalpine fir, and Douglas-fir. Shade-tolerant, like all climax species, Engelmann spruce of any size, from seedlings to mature specimens over 100 feet (30 meters) high, are found in the same stands.

Even the hardiest trees eventually yield to the cold, dryness, fierce winds, and thin soils of mountain terrain above the timberline. The boundary that marks the growth of normal-sized trees wanders up and down depending on the particularities of contour, exposure, and the presence of streams or tarns. There are islands of trees above timberline, as well as patches of meadows in the forests below.

Trees near timberline are dwarfed and twisted. Though small, many have survived longer than redwoods or firs a hundred times taller. Longest-lived is the bristlecone pine, a denizen of high alpine slopes. The ages of some trees in California's White Mountains exceed 4,000 years. At the upper limit of its growth, the bristlecone clings to stony ledges and windswept ridges, a gnarled, contorted shrub. Like the limber pine, juniper, subalpine fir, and other trees that survive in the alpine tundra, its form is shaped by the wind. The branches project outward from one side of the trunk, like flags waving in the breeze, making obvious the direction of prevailing winds. Not only does the wind dry out the tree's new buds, but it blasts them with sand and ice crystals, making twig development impossible. The leeward branches grow normally, becoming longer each year.

DURING THE FEW fleeting months of summer, the timberline region is a hub of activity. The growth of wildflowers and shrubs is frenzied, as each must flower and disperse its seeds in the shortest of seasons. Rapid plant growth provides a feast for animals, many of which must store enough fat to last them through the coming winter of hibernation. Black and grizzly bears pluck blueberries with their long, nimble lips, gaining about 10 pounds (4.5 kilograms) of fat for every 100 pounds (45 kilograms) of plant matter they consume. Others, such as pikas and chipmunks, are unable to build up sufficient fat reserves, and cache seeds, fruits, and dried grasses in burrows.

To conserve energy over the winter, a black bear's heart rate drops to only 10 beats per minute, 25 percent of the normal rate. Waste liquids are cleansed and recycled within its body for as long as three months to avoid loss of heat through urination. Chipmunks, except for brief visits to food caches every four or five days, pass the winter curled into cold balls, their body temperatures reduced to a few degrees above freezing. Despite this efficiency, alpine hibernators may lose half their body weight by the time they emerge in spring. Other animals are active year-round.

THE SONG OF an American dipper rolls out from the overhanging boughs of a juniper, following the course of the stream, layering its music atop the bubbling water. The bird appears, trailing after its song, a soft blur of wings sailing just above the stream. It lands on a shelf of ice, bobs up and down, and plunges from view.

The dipper lives the year-round in streams of the western mountains, feeding on small aquatic animals, such as insects, shrimp, snails, and fish. It walks on the stream bottom or flies through the water on stubby wings in search of its prey. Its aquatic adaptations are extraordinary for a songbird. To ensure adequate waterproofing, its preening gland, from which the bird extracts oil with its bill to spread over its feathers, is 10 times larger than that of its relatives. Splashes are kept out of its eyes by a special membrane and from its nostrils by a retractable flap.

Despite such departures from typical songbird anatomy, the dipper's voice is undeniably musical, and to be heard above the rush of mountain water, it is also powerful. The fluting melodies are not reserved just for the courtship rites of spring; the dipper sounds off every month of the year. The reasons are not clear, but to those familiar with its magic, it is embraced as an ode to the mountains and the forests where the dipper makes its home.

Mountain Forests

Grizzly bear.

Autumn larches at treeline, Kananaskis Country, Alberta.

THE DISTRIBUTION of tree species in the mountain forests is dependent on elevation, temperature, soil, and rainfall. Forest fires are frequent and initiate a predictable succession of regrowing species culminating in climax communities. Over much of the Rocky Mountain region, juniper and pinyon pine savannahs occupy the lowest slopes. Ponderosa pine and Douglas-fir are prominent in the mid-elevation montane forests. Higher up in the subalpine forests, lodgepole pine, Engelmann spruce, mountain hemlock, and subalpine fir are common. These species become dwarfed and twisted near timberline. Above this, even the hardiest species eventually yield to the cold, fierce winds, poor soil, and lack of moisture.

Trembling aspens, Red Rock Lakes National Wildlife Refuge, Montana.

*N*O DECIDUOUS *tree is more readily identified with the mountains than the trembling aspen. Long, limber leafstalks cause its leaves to quiver in the slightest breeze. In autumn the foliage turns gold, a dramatic contrast to the heavy greens of the ubiquitous conifers. Aspens grow rapidly, especially on sunny sites cleared by fire or logging. Here they often regenerate through root suckering, a process where new saplings shoot up from the roots of established trees, thereby avoiding the environmental stresses that seedlings face. These suckers grow rapidly, reaching 10 feet (3 meters) in only six to eight years. Such groves attract wildlife: elk congregate to browse on twigs and gnaw the bark, ruffed grouse feed on the buds and leaves, and varying hares eat the tender bark of younger trees.*

Varying hare.

Ponderosa pines, Coconiño National Forest, Arizona.

THROUGHOUT MOST of the Western Cordillera, the ponderosa pine is the most common tree at lower elevations. Higher up the slopes it gives way to Douglas-fir, lodgepole pine, and other conifers more tolerant of cold. Ponderosa pine thrives on sites too dry for other trees. The thick bark on mature specimens is resistant to the forest fires that sweep regularly through the dry montane zone. Stands of ponderosa pine are typically open so that individual trees may establish the wide-spreading root system necessary to gather adequate water and soil nutrients. Despite abundant sunlight, the understory vegetation is usually sparse, since few wildflowers, grasses, or shrubs can penetrate the thick layer of needle and cone debris that the trees cast off.

*T*HE CANYONS *and river
bottomlands of the western
mountains have a climate that is
generally warmer and drier than
habitats found upslope. The conifers
that dominate at higher elevations are
outnumbered here by broad-leaved
trees, both deciduous and evergreen.
Canyon live oaks, cottonwoods,
willows, and poplars line the watercourses. The canopy is usually open,
and enough light penetrates into the
understory to support grasses,
wildflowers, and numerous shrubs.
These riverine habitats provide food,
shelter, and reproductive sites for mule
deer, coyotes, and cottontails which
retreat to the thickets for protection
during the day, and owls, hawks, and
other birds, which nest in the trees.*

Red columbine, Manning Park, British Columbia.

Freemont cottonwoods, Zion National Park, Utah.

*T*HE SUBALPINE *forests,*
especially near timberline, are
interspersed with meadows. During
the short mountain summers, these
habitats sustain much plant and
animal activity. The brief growing
season requires that wildflowers grow
and bloom quickly with many different
species producing color simultaneously.
The melting snow pack provides plenty
of water, which is retained by soils that
have formed in depressions, along
streamsides and tarns, and on gentle
slopes. Here heathers, blueberries, and
lush grasses and herbs are frequently
more than waist high.

Sticky geranium, Yellowstone National Park, Wyoming.

Alpine sunflowers, Yellowstone National Park, Wyoming.

Subalpine forests, Columbia Mountains, British Columbia.

AS WITH trees, the distribution of shrubs in the mountain forests is mostly dependent on elevation. Near timberline and above, the crooked, straggling form of black mountain huckleberry is commonly found. Although at lower elevations it reaches shoulder height, it is less than a foot high in the uppermost reaches of its range. It often grows in the company of white moss heather and red mountain heather, two ground-hugging evergreens, which may carpet extensive stretches. Farther down the mountainside, the number of species increases. Here, the tangled branches of white rhododendron make each step a struggle for the hiker. Buffalo berry, a bushy, upright shrub whose fruits foam-up when rubbed, grows abundantly in forest openings. Other common shrubs are copper bush, grouse whortleberry, false azalea, kinnikinnick, and numerous blueberries, elderberries, currants, and raspberries, including thimbleberry.

Frosted thimbleberry, northern Idaho.

Fire-damaged pines and firs, Yellowstone National Park, Wyoming.

*F*IRE STRONGLY *influences the mountain forests. Severe lightning storms coincide with the summer dry season, often resulting in great destruction. Foresters estimate that every 200 to 300 years fires race through the spruce and lodgepole pine canopy found at higher elevations. On the lower, drier slopes, intermittent wildfires occur every 5 to 30 years. Fire changes the character of the forest, favoring pioneering species such as aspen and larch over climax species such as Douglas-fir and spruce. Some conifers such as lodgepole pine, produce cones that do not release their seeds unless subjected to the intense heat of a forest fire. Areas opened up by fire benefit bear, deer, elk, and other wildlife species that browse on the regrowing herbs, seedlings, and shrubs. Periodic fires also limit the spread of insect infestations and diseases. Throughout history man has either intentionally set forest fires or tried to stop them. Which practice is more beneficial for the forest remains a controversial issue.*

Douglas-fir and spruce forests along Thompson River, British Columbia.

Subalpine forests, Jasper National Park, Alberta.

Olympic marmot and Indian paintbrush.

*THE HIGH COUNTRY is
renowned for its wildlife. The
rugged terrain has limited human
encroachment on wildlife ranges, a
boon especially to larger species, such
as bear, deer, and moose. During the
summer's short but intense growing
season, many animals migrate into the
alpine regions to feed on the lush
vegetation. This is the only time of year
when most of the resident species, such
as ground squirrels, marmots, and
pikas, are active. The layered terrain,
open forests and meadows, and far-
reaching vistas make it easy to spot
wildlife. The overall impression during
summer is one of natural abundance;
however for nine months of the year,
the mountain world is a frozen, empty
place. The animals have either retreated
to the valleys or entered hibernation
underground. The large ungulates —
bighorn sheep, mountain goats, deer,
and elk — seek shelter in the dense
subalpine forests as winter sets in. They
gradually descend the mountainside to
escape the creeping cold and to reach
forage not buried in snow. When
summer returns, the squirrels emerge
from their burrows, the sheep climb out
of the valleys, and the slopes come alive
once more.*

Bighorn sheep.

Photography Notes

THE METHODS I USED for making the photographs in this book were simple. My equipment consisted of a standard 35 mm single-lens reflex camera, most recently the Canon T90. The lenses varied in focal length from 24 mm wide-angle to 300 mm telephoto. Usually I shot with zoom lenses adjusted to a focal length of around 100 mm. The zooms conveniently allowed me to achieve precise framing of the subject without having to reposition the tripod. For the leaf close-ups, I used a 100 mm macro lens, sometimes mounted on a bellows if extra magnification was needed.

Without exception, all exposures were made using a tripod — the Bogan 3021 with Bogan ball head 3055. The tripod provided for maximum sharpness by stabilizing the camera during exposure. The shutter was released by means of an electric cable, rather than manually, to avoid jarring the camera while the shutter was open.

Red maple leaves, Vermont.

When I first started working on these pictures more than 10 years ago, the finest grained film with the truest color was Kodachrome 25, which I used whenever possible. Often, however, my cameras were loaded with Kodachrome 64. Although not as detailed, it has a speed advantage desirable when shooting wildlife, a subject that preoccupied me at that time. About four years ago I began using Fujichrome 50 because it rendered color more vibrantly, although with less detail. This film was subsequently replaced two years ago by the finer-grained Fujichrome Velvia (ISO 50) which, compared with the Kodachromes, produces equal detail but exceeds them in color saturation.

A polarizing filter was used in making 90 percent of the pictures presented here. This filter removes the reflections from leaf surfaces, intensifying the color. For most scenes dominated by warm colors, I also attached an amber filter (1A), which further accentuated these tones.

In order to obtain sharpness throughout the scene, I chose a lens aperture that yielded maximum depth of field, normally opting for a setting of f/11 or f/16. Rarely did I give priority to shutter speed. In cases where the foliage was being disturbed by the wind, I sometimes chose a shutter speed slow enough (one to two seconds) to allow the leaves to become blurred on film in contrast to the trunks and large branches which remained sharp. Exposure was determined by the camera's thru-the-lens light meter which I usually set to take an average reading. From this basic setting I would take a series of extra pictures, one stop over and one stop under, at one-half stop increments.

I usually restricted the periods of photography to overcast days, the layer of clouds acting to diffuse the light from the sun, which allowed all parts of the scene to be evenly illuminated. Due to exposures lasting for one-fourth of a second or more, it was also necessary, unless I was attempting to achieve a blurred effect, that the foliage remain undisturbed by the wind. If such conditions did not materialize, I made the photographs during twilight — before sunrise or after sunset when it is usually calmer and the light is low in contrast. I often overexposed the scenes by one-half to a full stop to lower the contrast further, a condition that imparts a painterly quality to the photographs. Later I compensated for the attendant decrease in color intensity without altering the contrast by making corrections in the color separations prepared for printing, over which I had control.

The most exciting element of picture design for me is color. Consequently, I conducted many of the shooting sessions in the fall when the forests, particularly those in the East, were at their fiery best. I preferred periods later in the fall when about half the leaves had already dropped. With the forests more open, I was able to record views deeper into the trees and achieve a feeling of greater perspective. In addition, the dark trunks and branches, having lost much of their cover,

173

American beech, sugar maple, and yellow birch, Gatineau Park, Quebec.

contrasted strongly with the bright color of the foliage. I also enjoy the effects of fog, which generate a sense of mystery and accentuate the feeling of depth, a compelling design element when incorporated on a two-dimensional surface such as film.

The work on this book took place intermittently over a period exceeding 10 years, during which time I drove tens of thousands of miles, many of them along back roads. On countless occasions I would stop, haul tripod and camera bag out of the back of the car or van, hike into the woods 100 feet (30 meters) or so, and shoot a roll of film. With a particularly attractive subject, I would experiment with several setups,

trying different angles, magnifications, and lenses. Many of the photos were made during the course of day hikes along established trails. With experience, I came to rely on intuition in deciding which trees I would photograph and which ones I would pass by.

But the photographic process didn't end once I set down the camera. For me, the selective process continues over the light table, after the film has been developed. Needless to say, I have thousands of images of trees and forests that will never leave my slide files.

Bibliography

Arno, Steven F. 1977. *Northwest Trees.* Seattle: The Mountaineers.

Audubon, M.R. 1986. *Audubon and His Journals, Vol. II.* New York: Dover Publications.

Banfield, A.W.F. 1974. *The Mammals of Canada.* Toronto and Buffalo: University of Toronto Press.

Beasley, Jr., Conger, et al. 1984. *The Sierra Club Guides to the National Parks: Desert Southwest.* New York: Stewart, Tabori & Chang, Inc.

Behler, John L., and F. Wayne King. 1979. *The Audubon Society Field Guide to North American Reptiles and Amphibians.* New York: Alfred A. Knopf, Inc.

Belous, Robert, et al. 1981. *The Sierra Club Guides to the National Parks: Pacific Northwest and Alaska.* New York: Stewart, Tabori & Chang, Inc.

Brockman, Frank C. 1986. *A Guide to Field Identification: Trees of North America.* New York: Golden Press.

Brooks, Maurice. 1967. *The Life of the Mountains.* New York: McGraw-Hill Book Company.

Carr, E. 1966. *Hundreds and Thousands: The Journals of an Artist.* Toronto: Irwin Publishing.

Collingwood, G.H., and Warren Brush. 1984. *Knowing Your Trees.* Washington, D.C.: The American Forestry Association.

Howarth, William, et al. 1985. *America's Wild Woodlands.* Washington, D.C.: National Geographic Society.

Martin, Alexander C., Herbert S. Zim, and Arnold L. Nelson. 1961. *American Wildlife and Plants.* New York: Dover.

McCormick, Jack. 1966. *The Life of the Forest.* New York: McGraw-Hill Book Company.

McLaren, Christie. 1990. "Heartwood." *Equinox*, Number 53.

Miller, Jr., Orson K. 1979. *Mushrooms of North America.* New York: E.P. Dutton.

Milne, Lorus, and Margery Milne. 1980. *The Audubon Society Field Guide to North American Insects and Spiders.* New York: Alfred A. Knopf, Inc.

Muir, J. 1973. "Journal Entry on Mt. Rainier." In *The American Wilderness, In the Words of John Muir.* edited by Country Beautiful. Wisconsin: Country Beautiful.

Norton, Phillip. 1985. "Decline and Fall." *Harrowsmith*, Number 60.

Peattie, Donald Culross. 1950. *A Natural History of Trees.* Boston: Houghton Mifflin Company.

Petrides, George A. 1972. *A Field Guide to Trees and Shrubs.* Boston: Houghton Mifflin Company.

Smith, A.J.M. 1973. "The Lonely Land." In *Marked by the Wild,* edited by Bruce Litteljohn and Jon Pearce. Toronto: McLelland and Stewart.

Stevenson, George B. 1967. *Trees of the Great Smoky Mountains National Park.* Cosby, Tennessee: Published in Cooperation with The Great Smoky Mountains Natural History Association.

Sutton, Ann, and Myron Sutton. 1988. *The Audubon Society Nature Guides: Eastern Forests.* New York: Alfred A. Knopf, Inc.

Terres, John K. 1980. *The Audubon Society Encyclopedia of North American Birds.* New York: Alfred A. Knopf, Inc.

Whitney, Stephen. 1989. *The Audubon Society Nature Guides: Western Forests.* New York: Alfred A. Knopf, Inc.

Whitman, W. 1960. "Leaves of Grass." In *American Poetry and Prose.* edited by Norman Foerster and Robert Falk. Boston: Houghton Mifflin Company.

Zim, Herbert S., and Alexander C. Martin. 1956. *Trees: A Guide to Familiar American Trees.* New York: Golden Press.

PRODUCED BY TERRAPIN BOOKS

Managing Editor: Audrey Fraggalosch
Consulting Editor: Donald G. Bastian
Editorial Assistant: Melissa Jeter
Research Assistant: Star Rush
Scientific Reviewers: Dr. William J. Crins,
    John Farrand, Jr., Dr. Jerome Jackson
Art Director: Klaus Tyne
Drawings: Don Li-Leger
Cartography: Beverly Schrengohst
Typography: Marcus Yearout, Trish Lemon
Graphic Assembly: Vivian Reece
Production: Arnold Mann
Color Separations: Dong-A Printing